1000 HOURS OUTSIDE™
Activity Book

Low Tech
Nature Activities
in a High Tech
World

GINNY YURICH

1000 Hours Outside Activity Book:
Low Tech Nature Activities in a High Tech World
Copyright © 2021 by Ginny Yurich

Photographer: Ginny Yurich
Editor: Cathy Haddad

Cover design and book layout by Saint Creative, LLC
www.saint-creative.com

Correspondence and comments?
Write to Ginny at: Ginny@1000hoursoutside.com

This book is available at a discount for retail, wholesale, bulk and
promotional purchase. For more details, email hello@1000hoursoutside.com.

Printed in the United State of America
First Printing: Spring 2021

ISBN: 978-1-63848-445-5

To my five favorite kids - Jacko, Viv, Chooch, Brookie, and JoJo

ACTIVIY GUIDE

TABLE OF CONTENTS

INTRODUCTION

No one really tells you what to do with your kids once you have them. Sure, you're supposed to read to them and give them a bath and feed them, but what about all the rest of the time? How do you fill the minutes and hours that seem to stretch on toward eternity when they are small?

We started our parenting journey with enrollment, trying a bunch of different classes that were offered for infants and toddlers. It was exhausting to cart little people around to these short courses offered for enrichment. It also got pricey. Often we would return home from a program before lunch and I would already be exhausted from the packing and wrangling. Hours loomed until bedtime. The days were very overwhelming.

A turning point on our journey happened when a friend introduced me to the work of Charlotte Mason, an English educator and reformer born in 1842. She left us with her extensive philosophy on child-rearing and education. Included in her volumes of work is the charge for children to spend four to six hours outside "on any tolerable day."

This concept of nature immersion seemed absolutely absurd to me. I didn't know one other person who was choosing to spend their time in this way. Four to six hours was a far cry from the thirty to forty-five minute toddler classes we had been taking.

These words of Charlotte Mason, written over 100 years ago, came to life for us one fall day in Michigan. Our plan was to meet at a local park, just an open field without a play structure. We met up at nine in the morning and planned to stay until one o'clock in the afternoon, bringing only a picnic blanket and a picnic lunch.

I can attest that I had no idea what would happen. I thought the kids would instantly be bored. I had three wee ones, and so did my friend. What ensued was nothing short of miraculous. The kids played. And then they played some more. They chased squirrels, they jumped off stumps and rolled down hills and genuinely seemed thrilled with this open-ended freedom. This was the best day I had as a

mother up to that point, because it birthed in me hope that I could not only make it through these early years of child-rearing but that I could also thrive.

Our nature immersion day went so beautifully that we planned another and then another. At first, these days were solely for my benefit. The time outside gave me a sense of reprieve and they helped the hours of day float by a little easier. A few weeks passed and I began to notice some significant changes in my kids. They were healthier, more coordinated, and full of life.

It would be a few years before I would read about the things I had already seen happening within my own children. Without exception, every research report points to the incredible developmental gains that come hand-in-hand with nature play. In fact, time outdoors helps children grow in every facet of development including physical, emotional, social and cognitive. Interestingly, the time factor mirrors the original charge from Charlotte Mason. Recommendations ring in anywhere from three to eight hours of free play a day, preferably outside with variances based on age.

Despite the extensive research, kids are spending less time than ever outdoors. According to the National Wildlife Federation, the average American child only gets four to seven minutes worth of free play outside on a daily basis. That's not a typo. On the flip side, child screen use is on the rise with children ages eight to twelve often spending four to six hours a day watching or using screens while teenagers are on devices for up to nine hours each day. We've lost our balance.

1000 Hours Outside is a simple concept. Bring the balance back by including 1000 hours of outdoor time within one calendar year. You can begin this journey any time. Make it a goal to weave hands-on, real-world experiences through childhood to counteract a screen-heavy culture. If kids can consume media through screens 1200 hours a year, then the time is there. At least some of it can and should be shifted towards a more productive and healthy outcome.

Let's Begin!

If you are wanting to slow down and yet gain more through these swiftly moving years of childhood, all you need to do is add in some nature time. Pack up a first aid kit, some snacks and water, and maybe a spare outfit or two, and step outdoors. Breathe in the scents. Listen to the critters. Feel the breeze across your face. Watch the trees sway. And then step back as your children become immersed in the surroundings.

Nature is all around us. You do not need to visit an exotic land to find what kids are looking for. You don't even need your own yard. Children are fascinated by the ants on an ant hill, the lady beetle crawling across the balcony railing, and the weeds thrusting up through the cracks in the sidewalk. The activities you will find in this book incorporate the simple parts of nature that are abundant and full of variety; sticks, leaves, stones, flowers, water and the like.

No matter your geographic region or climate you will find plenty of worthwhile ventures within these pages. Watch for activities that overlap! Decorate your forest teepee with your wax-dipped leaves, twig stars, or hapa zome. Use your painted sticks to create your stick raft. These activities are all open-ended which means they should provide hours of entertainment and enjoyment for your family or classroom.

How to Use This Book

Kids are busy with important work. They are pruning their brains for maximum efficiency and they are discovering the world and themselves. The work of a child requires an immense amount of sensory input, which is one of the reasons child-rearing can be so exhausting!

Instead of turning to a screen, I've written this book to show how simple, open-ended nature activities can provide hours of enriching entertainment for a child. Each of the family-friendly activities in this book was carefully chosen to be developmentally beneficial, easily accessible, and delightful to participate in.

To encourage you on your journey, I've highlighted some of those benefits on certain activities. You can find a comprehensive list in the back of this book. Learn how interaction with nature helps children grow emotionally, academically, physically and socially. Participate in projects that help with fine-motor, large-motor, and creative enhancement. Knowing these benefits may give you a boost in your confidence to try these activities. I promise you'll see the engagement almost immediately!

We are trained to think that adult-directed activities provide children with the best learning opportunities. What is true for children, and indeed all people of any age, is that the learning that springs forth from self-interested pursuits tends to last a lifetime. The things that we learn that truly become a part of us can be used to scaffold new information which is why hands-on experiences give children such an academic advantage. As you introduce these activities, remember to let the child lead the way as much as possible. Be a spectator, a cheerleader and watch your child or your student construct knowledge through first-hand experiences.

Dive right in with the ones that look the most exciting. Include your child in the process of choosing. The supplies you will need, beyond some natural elements that can often be found right outside your door, are very minimal. They are items you can keep on hand as you enjoy these projects over and over again through the changing seasons of the year. As a family, we can't wait to do all of these activities again!

INTRODUCTION

Tracker Sheet

The amount of time kids spend outside matters, though you may not hear this very often. At first this may seem cumbersome, another thing to add to the ever-growing list of a parent or caregiver. But truly, this is great news! Outdoor play gives back in ways you could never even imagine, both for the child and the grown-up.

As you work through the delightful activities in this book and find yourself outside collecting natural materials, building forts, or playing in a mud kitchen, you can begin to record your outside time on a 1000 Hours Outside tracker sheet. These tracker sheets are available for free on the 1000 Hours Outside website, www.1000hoursoutside.com . Color in one circle or one section for every hour spent outside. Include the child in your recordings! This is a tangible way to model balance to children in an increasingly tech-saturated world.

The 1,000 Hours Outside journey is a global movement to encourage parents, caregivers, and teachers, to get children outside for 1,000 hours every calendar year throughout childhood. This quest is meant to restore the hands-on moments kids need to thrive while living in a world increasingly bent toward virtual experiences. Since many of the activities in this book are open-ended, they will get you well on your way to achieving 1,000 hours outside and a balanced childhood!

Nature Exploration

Kids are naturally curious. They are born mini-scientists. Driven by instinct they will prod, poke, squeeze, smell, and even taste the nature elements that are around them. With each of these actions they are hypothesizing in their minds. What will happen if I stomp in this puddle of water? How far will this rock go if I throw it? Can I break this stick with my hands? Each action feeds information back through the brain and as it is with all hands-on activities, they are learning.

The more senses we engage, the more a child will learn. Nature activities often engage several senses at once which is why real-life experiences are so powerful for children. This book is flush with those types of activities that leave children occupied and wide-eyed. Nature is enthralling. When we watch one seed slowly turn into a vine that produces not just one, but several juicy melons we are changed. It is like witnessing a miracle. A sunflower that stretches to the sky and so quickly becomes out of reach leaves us all in awe. The forest floor is filled with endless possibilities. So too, a tiny backyard and a small neighborhood park.

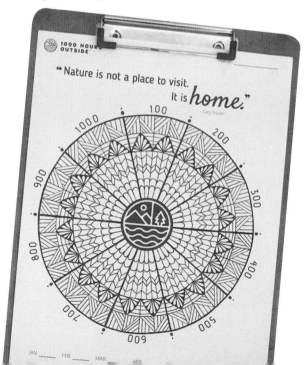

For Parents, Teachers and Caregivers

As parents and educators, we are in a well-intentioned pursuit of raising whole children. Yet we are missing this key element of nature exposure while simultaneously being inundated with virtual experiences. It feels nice to have a systematic approach to childhood. It is reassuring to check off boxes of standards and accomplishments. In a world where there is a lot of pressure to push children to succeed academically, it can be hard to remember that simply interacting with nature provides kids with a multitude of benefits.

Open-ended nature time can make adults feel a little bit uneasy. When kids play, and especially when they play outside, they are learning a tremendous amount of things we may not be easily able to measure or track. If you feel a little leary about spending your time this way, remember that self-constructed knowledge tends to last and it provides a foundation for all other learning in the future. The activities that follow in this book will help guide you into the situations that fill childhood with beauty, wonder, learning experiences, joy, and memories you will always look back on fondly.

FOREST DWELLERS

Nature's Sanctuary Amidst the Trees

There's no telling what you will find when you head into the woods:
a bright red mushroom, a spotted salamander, a perfectly symmetrical web of a spider, a blossom, a bunny! There is a sense of excitement every time we enter the woods because we don't know what we will encounter.

In the pages to come, you will find ideas to utilize on your hiking journeys and once your journey. Often children return home with pockets full of goodies. A hike can be as short as a walk around a pond or as long as several miles or more. If you are new at this, start small and work up your stamina. Remember to stay safe! There is safety in numbers. It's always important to let a loved one know where you are headed, especially if there is little cell-service at your destination.

Don't have a small forest nearby? No worries! All of these activities can be adapted to local areas filled with nature items. In most cities and countrysides you will be able to find plenty of sticks and other loose parts in nature. Be sure you have permission to remove a few items from wherever you are visiting.

Get ready for some hands-on, real-life memories!

Journey Stick

Hiking gets kids and adults of all ages outside and moving. Add an extra special touch to your hike with a journey stick. Your journey stick will remind you of the memories you made and things you saw along the trail.

TIME: 5 minutes to prepare
Use for as long as you'd like on your hike

SUPPLIES:

*Hiking size stick - a good size for children is generally around 41 inches (104 cm) and a good size for adults is around 55 inches (140 cm)

*Twine, colorful yarn or rubber bands

*Extras such as bells or dried fruit slices, optional

*Scissors, optional

INSTRUCTIONS:

1. Wrap twine or colorful yarn all the way down your stick and then back up to the top, tying the two ends together once they meet. Alternatively, you could wrap rubber bands beginning at the top of your stick and going down to the bottom about two inches (5 cm) apart.

2. Start with a little something special tied onto your journey stick if you wish. You could begin with a few jingle bells or some pretty dried fruit slices and tie them to your twine, yarn or secure with rubber bands before you even start out on your hike. These items add some extra sensory fun with the sound of the bells and the citrusy smells of the fruit slices.

3. Along your hike stop to collect nature treasures and affix them to your journey stick. You can use some additional yarn or twine to tie them onto your stick or you could slide your items in between the material you've used and the stick itself. Rubber bands make

this process even easier as the child can just slide in the special collectibles by stretching the rubber band just a little bit to fit the nature treasure in.

TAKE IT FURTHER:
When you add items to your journey stick consider placing them in a certain order, either from bottom to top or from top to bottom. Once your hike is over use your journey stick to retell the places you've been and the adventures you've had along the way. Consider making a journey stick for each season at your favorite hiking location. This is also an easy activity to incorporate the summer and winter solstices. Use this as an opportunity to talk about how the plant life changes from week to week and month to month. Which journey stick is your favorite? Which is the most colorful? Which is the least colorful? Do certain seasons offer more nature treasure options to find?

PARK RULES:
Make sure to read up on park rules before removing anything from its natural surroundings. Some parks may allow you to pick up nature items along the way but require you to put them back. Other parks may want you to leave the natural landscape as it is. In this case, you could do a journey walk and take photographs of things that are of key interest. Children have a natural affinity for collecting things, so be sure and know the rules ahead of time.

Time:
20 min

Twig Star

Left to the imagination sticks can turn into almost anything, making them one of nature's most used toys. Piecing together twig stars is a great workout for fine motor skills. Once completed, twig stars make whimsical decor for your forest den, teepee, bedroom, and more!

TIME: 20 minutes after you've collected your sticks

SUPPLIES:

*Five or six sticks fallen sticks that are all approximately the same length

*Twine or yarn

*Heated glue dispenser, optional

*Glue sticks for heated glue dispenser, optional

INSTRUCTIONS:

1. Collect five or six fallen sticks of approximately the same length. The bigger the sticks you choose, the bigger your star will be.

2. Lay out your sticks in your favorite star shape. You could make a five pointed star, sometimes called a golden five pointed star. Or you could make a six pointed star by beginning with two triangles. If you make a six pointed star be sure to interweave your triangles and tie twine or yarn in the spots where the triangles overlap each other.

3. At each of the corners wrap twine or yarn around both sticks several times and in several directions. Once the corners are secure tie them and cut off the extra bits of twine or yarn. If the sticks move around too much for little hands, try connecting your twigs into the shape of a star with heated glue and then wrapping the corners once the glue has dried completely.

KID DECORATOR IDEAS: Think about some different places you could hang your stars as decorations? Is there an outside tree you can hang them on? How about along a fence post? Would they look pretty hanging on your front door or in a window? Which colors of yarn could you use to make your stars perfect for the season you are in? Experiment with different sizes of stars. Small ones could be used on birthday packages. Large stars could be used inside of wreaths. You can even paint your stars! Start with painted twigs or paint your star once it is complete.

Did you know? 35 countries have at least one five pointed star in their flags. Is yours one of them?

Academic benefits: The study of stars provides an avenue for all sorts of learning in the realms of both science and math. Use this project as a jump-start to talking about constellations. By experimenting with twig stars made of different amounts of sticks you can begin to discuss angles and names of polygons.

Magic Wand

Bring out your inner wizard or fairy with a magic wand made out of a stick. There are endless possibilities here for creativity. These could be made any time of the year and used over and over again in pretend play.

TIME: 20 - 40 minutes

SUPPLIES:

*Stick

*Ribbon or yarn

*Scissors

*Glue or tape

*Natural decor such as leaves or acorns

*Beads, optional

INSTRUCTIONS:

1. Find a stick that you love. Hunt for one with special characteristics such as unique coloring or interesting knots. Your stick can be straight or it can be curved. Anything goes! Just make sure it fits perfectly in your hand.

2. Gather your favorite magical materials such as ribbon, yarn, and other natural decor.

3. Check the bark status of your stick. If it has loose bark, try and peel it off before creating your wand.

4. Wind some wool or yarn around your stick. Consider winding in a special pattern such as criss-cross or alternating between colors. You could even make a pattern with the colors that you choose. Either make a knot at the very beginning or wind all the down the wand and then back up, making your knot at the very end.

5. Add some natural decor to your wand using glue or tape. One of the most special places to decorate is at the end of your wand. Use one of the most unique things you have to affix right at the end. Adding a few dangling ribbons to the end of your wand will make it extra fun to spin around. Small beads can be strung through the ribbon as well.

TAKE IT FURTHER:
Try making an ice wand! Fill any type of small bowl or mold with water. Add coloring if desired. Place your stick straight up in the center of the mold or bowl and use two sticks on either side to hold it in place. Freeze either outside or in the freezer and decorate once frozen. You could do this with a wand you have already wound with yarn or ribbon just be sure to leave space at the end for your frozen piece.

4.

5.

Time:
60 min

Twig-Bound Journal

Nature journaling provides us with so many benefits. Young children can use these twig-bound homemade journals to draw or paint while older children can use the journals to record nature adventures. Homemade journals also make beautiful gifts.

TIME: 60 minutes

SUPPLIES:

*One beautiful twig approximately six inches long

*Watercolor or cardstock paper

*Water color paints, wax crayons, markers, or another favorite art medium

*Drawing or printer paper

*Hole punch

*Rubber band

INSTRUCTIONS:

1. Fold your watercolor or cardstock paper in half. This will be the cover of your journal.

2. Decorate the front and the back of your journal using water colors, wax crayons, markers or your favorite art medium. Make sure your cover is completely dry before moving on. [QY0872_051]

3. Take your drawing or printer paper and fold it in half, placing it inside the cover.

4. Using your hole punch, punch one hole close to the top of your journal and one hole closer to the bottom of your journal along the folded edge, making sure the holes go through both sides of the cover and each of your inside sheets. Be careful not to spread your holes farther apart than your rubber band will be able to stretch. If your journal is too thick, take the inside pages out and hole punch them separately.

5. Loop your rubber band over one end of the twig and pull the rubber band down through the top whole of the journal, all the way through the inside pages and out the back. Take the rubber back down the back of the journal and out through the bottom whole toward the front, looping the bottom of the twig and securing it to the journal. [QY0872_050]

NATURE JOURNAL IDEAS:
*Animal track sketches
*Nature poetry
*Leaf or tree bark rubbings
*Nature stamps
*Nature observation lists such as insects, birds, plants or flowers
*Nature quotes
*Journal entries of hikes or other nature adventures
*Nature critter drawings

GIFT IDEA: Twig bound nature journals make great gifts, party favors, or nature group activities! You can make them in any size, even pocket size, depending on the size of paper you use.

EMOTIONAL HEALTH AND WELL-BEING:
Beyond being relaxing and enjoyable, expressing ourselves through art can help us emotionally as well. A study from the Frontiers in Human Neuroscience suggests that the creative process can stimulate the release of dopamine. Since journaling is also a great exercise for emotional health, the combination of journal creation and nature journaling is a powerful one.

Painted Sticks

Nature provides us with many interesting objects to paint on and an easy one to find is sticks. Kids love this hands-on, messy activity that stimulates their creativity and helps engage their fine-motor skills. From elaborate paintings on driftwood to some simple stripes on a twig, there are options for everyone to use their imaginations and get creative!

TIME: 15 - 45 minutes

SUPPLIES:

*Sticks of different lengths

*Paint

*Washi or painter's tape, consider using different widths

*Paintbrushes

*Glitter, optional

INSTRUCTIONS

1. Using washi tape or painter's tape wrap some bands around your stick that will stay clean when you paint. Think of different patterns you can make with your tape.

2. Paint in between your taped spots. Once again, consider different design ideas. Do you want to use all of the same color or alternate colors? Do you prefer darker colors or lighter colors? Which stands out more? If your stick has little twists and knobs you might want to paint those differently than the rest of the stick.

3. Wait until your first coat of paint has dried. If you paint isn't dark enough then paint a second coat. When you are satisfied with what you have, carefully unroll your tape and decorate the areas that haven't been painted with polka dots, wavy lines, stripes and other patterns. You can even add some glitter!

4. Let the paint dry completely.

5. Finished sticks look great in the garden bed. They can also be used to make stick mobiles or in some of your other twig crafts such as the twig stars, magic wand, and the twig-bound journal. Several painted sticks look pretty tied together and placed in a vase!

CHANGE IT UP: Use the sticks as paint brushes! Lay out a sheet of paper such as butcher paper. Instead of painting on the sticks use the sticks to paint a design on your paper. Which types of sticks are easiest to paint with? Which ones are hardest?

USE THESE LATER: A painted stick might make a great mast for your stick raft, use four painted sticks for the frame of your nature loom, bind your twig-bound journal with a painted stick, or use painted sticks to decorate your flower pot! You can hang several painted sticks from another stick to make a mobile. If you hang your mobile outdoors, the breeze will cause the sticks to strike together to make sounds like a wind chime.

2.

3.

Mud Faces

Mud and creativity go hand-in-hand! Combine the sensations of squishy mud with the thrill of creating something unique in this simple, yet engaging activity. This one works the fine motor skills as well as the imagination!

TIME: 5 - 60 minutes

SUPPLIES:

*Mud

*Loose parts from nature

*Tree or fence post

*Water, soap and towels for clean up

INSTRUCTIONS:

1. Find some nearby mud or make your own combining soil and water. Your mud should be a thick enough consistency to stick onto tree bark or a fence post. If it is too runny you won't be able to get it to stick to your surface.

2. Form a thick, fistful of mud into the shape of a patty and put your glob of mud on a tree or fence post, trying to maintain the shape of a patty. Be sure and choose a spot that is not being used by other living creatures and one that is also free of insects. If the mud patty starts to fall off, make sure to press it against the tree with your fingers. [QY0872_167]

3. Collect some loose parts from nature and use those to create a face on your mud circle. You could use bright flowers, leaves, small stones, seedlings, twigs, nuts and berries, pinecones, fuzzy moss and more!

4. Use your natural treasures to turn your mud patty into a face! You can add things like eyes, ears, a nose, a mouth, a beard, hair, or even a wart. Once you've made one, make another. Try creating a self-portrait or a portraits of friends, family, book characters, or even pets. Use your imagination to consider how that tree might be feeling and create a face that represents the personality of that specific tree.

5. Use water, soap and towels to clean up when you are finished.

6. Return after a few days and see if your mud face is still there. If it is still there, has anything changed?

TAKE IT FURTHER: Have your tree face tell a story! What special events has your tree seen in its lifetime? What is something exciting that has happened to your tree? Can you draw a picture of your mud face and then write an accompanying story in your nature journal? Think of what other creations you can make using mud and natural materials. How about adding a face to a large rock? You can also do this activity during different seasons, sometimes using snow instead of mud.

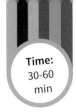

Nature Weaving

Nature weaving is a free activity that encourages children to explore the colors and textures of nature. Weaving is also a great choice for working on fine motor skills. Whatever you find outdoors becomes a delightful object to try and weave into your loom.

TIME: 30 - 60 minutes

SUPPLIES:

*Four sticks of approximately the same size that are about ¼" to ¾" (0.6 to 2 cm) in diameter

*Twine or yarn

INSTRUCTIONS:

1. Lay your sticks on in the shape of a square. If you'd like your nature loom to be more of a rectangular shape, make sure two of the sticks are longer than the other two.

2. Connect each corner with yarn or twine. Wrap the yarn using a criss-cross motion around the two sticks, pull tight, and then tie it off in the back. This will be your nature loom!

3. Take your yarn or twine and begin to wrap it around and around your loom, double wrapping on each side in order to prevent slipping. Keep your yarn or twine taut so that it will be easy to hold the nature items you weave in.

4. Head out on a nature walk to collect flowers, feathers, long grasses, twigs, weeds, and more.

5. Weave your collected items into your loom, over and under the twine. You can alternate directions to give it more variety.

TAKE IT FURTHER:
Experiment with different nature loom shapes and sizes. Can you make a triangular loom? How about a rectangular loom? Are you able to make a loom that is the shape of a hexagon? Can you find a stick that is already in the shape of a Y, string your yarn or twine back and forth between the top of the letter, and weave your nature items into the Y-shaped stick? An alternative to using sticks as the base for your nature loom is to use a piece of cardboard, cut slits in opposing sides, and wrap your yarn or rubber bands through the slits creating taut parallel lines of materials that you can weave your nature items in and out of.

FINE MOTOR SKILLS BENEFITS: Fine motor development activities help strengthen the muscles that are needed for writing and other academic pursuits. This activity helps children work the fine muscles of the hand and strengthen their pincer grip while also allowing them to feel a variety of different shapes and textures.

Lantern Hike

There is something magical about being outside after dark. There are lots of options to light your way like a headlamp or a flashlight but a small lantern is an enchanting way to light just a little bit of the path ahead of you. Make your own lantern and use it to entice your family outdoors for an adventure underneath the stars.

TIME: 30 - 60 minutes

SUPPLIES:

*Mason jar or other glass jar, with lid

*Mason jar lantern kit with firefly lights or bendable aluminum wire with a battery powered tealight

*Assorted tissue paper in different colors

*Foam brush

*Craft glue like Mod Podge

*Stencils, optional

INSTRUCTIONS:

1. Unscrew the lid of your mason jar or other glass jar and set it aside.

2. Cover the outside glass on your jar with a thick layer of watered down craft glue like Mod Podge. You can make your own watered down craft glue using a mixture of half glue and half water.

3. Attach different pieces of colored tissue paper to the outside of your jar. You can use your tissue paper to make clever designs. You can rip your paper into smaller pieces. You can cover the entire jar or leave some places blank where the glue will dry. You can also cut your tissue paper into shapes like trees or stars and create an entire outdoor scene on your lantern. Use stencils for this part, if you'd like.

4. Press your tissue paper down firmly onto the glue on your mason jar, especially around the edges of each piece so they won't curl up or move.

5. Once you have finished your design, let it dry.

6. Once your design is dry, cover the entire tissue paper design with a final thin layer of Mod Podge and leave that to dry for a few hours.

7. Insert the firefly lights from your lantern kit or a battery powered tealight.

8. Reattach the lid. If you bought a lantern kid your lid will already have a handle. If you are using aluminum wire, make a loop that attaches securely under the bottom ring of the mason jar. Cut your wire and create a small handle that wraps around from one side of the loop to the other. Be sure to test your handle for safety since the jars are made of glass. Alternately, you can use pipe cleaners or even twine to create a handle, but once again ensure that the handle is completely secure before using it as a lantern.

9. Use your lantern to explore at dusk or at night.

ALTERNATIVE DECORATING IDEAS:

*Use bits of wildflowers or leaves to decorate your lantern instead of tissue paper.

*Consider making seasonal lanterns with different nature component decor each season.

*Make color-themed lanterns using one color of tissue paper and matching nature items.

Forest Teepee

Children are drawn to secret spaces where they can let their imaginations run wild. A small teepee will provide hours of entertainment throughout the building process and beyond. A forest is a great place to build a teepee because you will find lots of natural materials to use however, you can make a teepee anywhere!

SUPPLIES:

*Sticks, lots of sticks

*Gardening gloves to protect your hands, optional

*A large supporting tree, optional

*Twine

*Scissors

INSTRUCTIONS:

1. The easiest way to build a teepee out of sticks is to begin with a large supporting tree. If you do not have one available you can start with three large sticks, prop them together in a tripod shape, and secure the top with twine. With this method, gently press your three sticks into the earth to give them more stability. Alternatively, you could find three large sticks that have a y-shape at the top and prop them up against each other.

2. Once you've determined how you will begin, either with a large supporting tree or three shapes in a triangular shape, gather your long branches and lean them up on an angle all around the tree trunk or your beginning stick shape. As you are placing your sticks you can make them extra secure by propping other bits of nature, such as logs or mud in front of them. Another way to keep them from moving is to push them right into the earth if the ground is soft enough. Once you have five to seven main supporting sticks in place, tie them securely around the top with twine. As your structure starts to take shape make sure to leave a small opening for a door.

3. When you have all of your larger sticks in place you can fill in any openings with smaller sticks, weaving them through side to side to add extra support.

4. Adorn with leaves, flowers, a homemade bunting, or your hapa zome creations!

TAKE IT FURTHER:

*Could you take this same activity and make it mini? Experiment with building a teeny teepee just the perfect size for woodland fairies and other magical creatures.

HEAVY WORK: Heavy work is any type of activity that pushes or pulls against the body. The resistance that happens during heavy work to the joints, muscles and connective tissues sends signals to the brain and helps children develop their proprioceptive system. In turn, this helps with body awareness. The process of moving large sticks and positioning them to create a teepee structure is a great example of a heavy work activity.

1.

4.

CHAPTER 2

GARDEN TINKERERS

Nature's Variety to Mesmerize the Senses

Our brains are wired for novelty. We gravitate towards things that are new to us because they have a tendency to make us happy, activating the pleasure centers of the brain. The garden is a place that satisfies this need for the unfamiliar. You can plant flowers, trees, vegetables, and fruits. There are lots of options here!

There are an estimated 400,000 flowering plant species. Let's say you pick zinnias. Zinnias are easy to grow, they produce stunning flowers for months, and they come in every color but blue! You could plant dwarf zinnias such as "Thumbelina Mix" or tall zinnias such as "Giant Cactus". There are over 1,000 types of vegetables and 2,000 types of fruits and just like the flowers, you could plant Tigger Melons or Moon & Stars Melons.

Garden seeds can be started inside and watching the first little sprouts poke out of the soil is thrilling. Some grow quicker than others and seedlings come in all shapes like the beautiful star shaped leaves of the lupine to the heart shaped leaves of the radish. Once securely placed in a garden bed, some plants climb up posts while others creep along the ground. It's a perpetual game of hide-and-seek, searching under leaves to find what might be growing.

From sprout to harvest to saving the seeds for next season, the garden is a place of endless delight.

Seed Bombs

Send seed bombs flying into an open meadow, plant them along the edge of a garden bed, or wrap them up beautifully as a gift. Check out the prices on these, save some money and make your own. Seed bombs are even given out as party favors at a wedding or baby shower. There is an element of surprise here that makes seed bombs an exciting activity. Plant your seed bombs just before heavy rainfall for optimal success.

TIME: 30 minutes / 3 hours to dry

SUPPLIES:

*Wildflower seed mix or seeds collected from the garden

*Clay powder for pottery

*Peat-free compost

*Water

*Mixing Bowl

*Baking tray

INSTRUCTIONS:

1. In your mixing bowl, mix together one handful of seeds with three handfuls of clay powder and five handfuls of compost.

2. Slowly add water to your mixture until everything sticks together. Be sure to add your water slowly because you don't want your mixture to be too goopy.

3. Once you've reached a desired consistency, roll your mixture into balls about the size of truffles and lay them on your baking sheet.

4. Allow your seed bombs to sit for at least three hours in a sunny location before using them or packaging them up.

5. Seed bombs are designed for adverse conditions but you should still be mindful of when and where you disperse them. In early spring or late fall, find a space that is clear of most weeds. Plant your seed bombs in a place where they will get water and moderate temperatures. If you can time your planting with a heavy rainfall, it will give your seeds a better chance of survival. The rain will cause the seed bomb to slowly dissolve and the seeds will begin germinating.

6. Instead of planting your seed bombs in the ground, you can also throw them or even shoot them off into different directions with a slingshot. These latter two options might be the preferred options for children. Seed bombs also make a great gift, packed in a small sack. Be sure they are completely dried before packing up so that they don't mold.

TAKE IT FURTHER: Create your own wildflower seed mix using seeds from flowers that pollinators love such as coneflower, snapdragon, sunflower, coreopsis, lupine, and foxglove. You can even add some edibles into your seed bombs such as radish, spinach or kale.

Supplies

2.

3.

6.

2.

DIY Flower Holder

Often the simplest of things can bring so much joy, satisfaction, beauty and entertainment. This may be one of the simplest activities in this book but it will lead to loads of play time. Gift a flower holder to a friend or neighbor, or use them in your flower farm stand.

TIME: 5 minutes

SUPPLIES:

*Wooden board at least two inches (five cm) thick

*Drill

*Flowers or weeds with stems

*Scissors

INSTRUCTIONS

1. Drill holes into your wooden board without going all the way through the wood. You can space these holes out however you would like. You can keep the holes in a straight line, zigzag them, or place them randomly.

2. Fill the holes with your flowers and weeds. Experiment with different heights. Do you like a uniform look or heights that are varied? Can you place your flowers and weeds in rainbow color order?

TAKE IT FURTHER: Consider adding a dazzling array of flowers to your DIY flower holder and giving it as a gift. Or you could use your flower holder in your flower farm display. Since these are so quick to make, you could have several flower holders at your flower farm. Choose one to hold pink flowers, one to hold yellow flowers and so on. Of all of the flower colors, did you know that blue is the color least likely to be found in a garden? Blue is the rarest flower color on earth. Only 10% of the 280,000 varieties of flowers are blue.

THE FLOWER COLOR WHEEL:
Colors have cultural associations as well as effects on human behavior. While choosing your flower colors read through the following commonly associated emotions and see if you agree!
Red - high energy
Pink - love
Orange - optimism
Yellow - joy
Green - growth
Blue - peace
Purple - imagination
White - freshness

Pocket-Sized Flower Press

You can easily preserve some of the beauty of your garden with a flower press. Pressed flowers can be used to add color to all sorts of crafts and projects through the year. You can buy a flower press but it's extra special to make your own! This one is pocket sized and perfect to take along on your outdoor adventures. Use your pressed flowers in some of the other projects in this book such as suncatcher, nature mandala, mud kitchen and flower pressed pinched clay bowls.

TIME: 45 minutes

SUPPLIES:

*One piece of cardstock, 8.5" x 11" (21.6 x 30 cm)

*Two pieces of cardboard, 4" by 10" (10.2 x 25.4 cm)

*One piece of felt, 12" by 11" (30.5 x 30 cm)

*Scissors

*Glue

*Two sets of circular hook and loop stickers

*Tape, optional

*Scraps of felt, optional

INSTRUCTIONS:

1. Fold your cardstock in half making a solid crease at 5.5" (14 cm).

2. Reopen your cardstock and glue one piece of cardboard on each side.

3. On each side of cardboard place a piece of wax paper that matches the side of the cardboard. Glue or tape if desired.

4. Place one set of hook and loop stickers on the top inside corners of the cover of your flower press and place the other set of hook and loop stickers on the bottom inside corners of the cover of your flower press. [QY0872_187]

5. Decorate the front of your flower press with felt scraps, if desired. [QY0872_186]

TIPS FOR PRESSING FLOWERS:

*Collect flowers on a sunny day when they are fully dry.

*Choose flowers that have recently bloomed. These will give the most vibrant colors.

*Flowers that lay flat naturally are the easiest to press. For larger flowers, such as roses or orchids, cut them down the middle with a knife or a pair of scissors. You can also press individual petals to use in crafts later on.

*Place a heavy book or other heavy object on your press while your flowers are drying out.

*Wait seven to ten days before checking on your pressed flowers and do not disturb in the meantime.

*Remove one set of pressed flowers before adding a new set. Since pressed flowers are often very delicate you can use tweezers to remove them if needed.

*If you have flowers you would like to press but can't press them right away, store them in the refrigerator inside of a sealed, plastic bag.

*Press other things besides flowers. Grasses, ferns, herbs and foliage can also be pressed. Pressed herbs can hold on to their aroma for years and years!

4.

5.

3.

Flower Farm Pretend Play

Flower bouquets bring a lot of joy but they are also delightful to make. It is fun to experiment with different sizes and textures of flowers, weeds, and grasses - combining them to form something exquisite. With just a smattering of materials, children can engage in hours of pretend play with their flower farm.

TIME: 15 - 30 minutes of set-up

SUPPLIES:

*Table or other flat surface

*Tablecloth, optional

*A variety of flowers, long grasses, and weeds

*Scissors

*Twine

*Watering cans

*Assorted vases or other containers that will hold water and/or small baskets

*Rectangular piece of wood and paint, optional

*Play money box with pretend money, optional

INSTRUCTIONS:

1. Set up your supplies trying to make it as whimsical as possible. Include your kids on this step. You can use a tablecloth, hang up a banner behind your flower farm, and even create a flower farm sign with your rectangular wooden board and paint. You could also use your wooden board to list your flower farm prices.

2. Take your gathered materials and set them up on your table. Fill your watering can and vases with water. Arrange your flowers, long grasses and weeds out on your table, in your vases, or in your baskets.

3. Invite friends, family and grandparents to come play along! Create all sorts of flower bouquets using scissors, twine and vases.

FLOWER ARRANGEMENT TIPS:

*Think about height. Your flower arrangement should be two and half times taller than the vase you are using, at its tallest point. Here's an excellent opportunity to work on a little math!

*Cut your stems on a 45o angle to allow the stems to continue to soak up water properly.

*Remove excess leaves from your stems because the leaves can collect bacteria and shorten the shelf-life of your floral arrangement.

*Use a little wire to support heavy blooms.

*Choose only a few focal points of the arrangement that really dazzle the eye. Less is more! Picking anywhere from one to five unique and spectacular flowers is enough to showcase your creation.

 *If you choose an arrangement that is monochromatic, make sure to use a variety of flowers with different shapes and textures.

*Think of alternate vase ideas. Could you repurpose a tin can or use a water pitcher for your floral arrangement?

Garden Markers

Garden markers are dual purpose. They help you identify what you've planted, especially if you've planted several varieties of the same thing. They also add a little whimsy to the garden. There are so many different options here. Try a variety of different kinds to learn what you like best.

TIME: 30 - 45 minutes

SUPPLIES:

*Rocks, twigs, large craft sticks or paint stirring sticks

*Acrylic paint

*Acrylic sealer

*Paint brushes

*Paint pens, optional

*Puffy paint, optional

INSTRUCTIONS:

1. Paint one side of your object if it will be laying flat in the garden (such as a rock) or both sides if it will be sticking out of the soil (such as a stick).

2. Allow the paint to dry and cover with sealer.

3. Decorate your sticks with words or pictures to convey what you've planted in this space.

4. Once your marker is fully dry place it in your garden and watch your seedlings grow. Depending upon the size of your garden marker you can use the height to determine how quickly your plants are growing.

5. Get creative! Look around you and see if there are other items you can repurpose as garden markers. A little bit of paint and some paint pens will go a long way. How about some canning lids, clothespins, kitchen utensils, bricks, cork stoppers, or even some plastic toy figurines? Wouldn't a child love it if a toy dinosaur showed them where the radishes were, or a toy lion marked the spot for the beets?

KIDS IN THE GARDEN: There are many multi-faceted benefits that coincide with spending time in a garden. Remember that a garden doesn't have to be a huge plot of land. It can be a few containers on a porch or some herbs on a windowsill.

Gardening in any form involves all the senses of a child. The more senses we engage, the more we learn! Additionally, the gardening process includes all sorts of scientific discoveries.

Here are some ways to easily include children in the garden:

*Let them plan their own small plot.

*Allow them to choose some of their own seed varieties

*Let them do the planting, watering, and harvesting.

*Make a scarecrow together.

*Create your own compost pile.

*Build a teepee for your beans and peas to grow up along.

4.

Seed Starting

Watching seeds germinate is a thrilling experience. There is immense variety in shape and size of both seeds and seedlings. Lots of hands-on learning happens when you get your hands in a little bit of dirt. Plop in a few seeds, and wait for the magic to happen.

TIME: 30 minutes

SUPPLIES

*Any type of container with drainage holes or a seed-starting tray. Your container could be a pot but an old yogurt container that you've cut a few holes out of the bottom would also work. Even egg cartons and plastic cups can be used! There are many options to use when starting seeds, including recycled ones. The drainage holes will help the seeds from becoming too soggy. Think about what you have lying around your home and save different receptacles throughout the year to plant your seeds in.

*Seeds. Certain seeds are easier than others to start indoors. If you're just beginning, consider trying tomatoes, marigolds, zinnias, basil or nasturtium. Sunflower seeds sprout up quickly but can be finicky to transplant.

*Seed-starting mix which is different from your garden soil. A seed-starting mix actually contains no soil at all and using this will help you avoid introducing potential disease spores right at the beginning. The seed-starting mix will say something like "soilless mix" or "sterile seed starting mix" on the bag.

*Water

*Light

INSTRUCTIONS:

1. Fill your containers with seed-starting mix and mist it so that it is moist but not sopping wet.

2. Before you begin, consider your timing. You will want to have your seedlings ready to be transplanted outside once the weather is favorable in your area.

3. Plant your seeds according to the depth written on the seed packet. If you don't have instructions the general rule of thumb is to plant a seed about two to three times as deep as a seed is wide. Tiny seeds should barely be covered with soil while larger sunflower seeds, for instance, should be planted an inch deep or so. Seeds that are sown too deeply won't have enough stored energy to make it up to the surface.

4. Plant at least two seeds per container because not every seed with germinate.

5. After you've sown your seeds, set your containers in a warm location and check daily for signs of growth. If the seed-starting mix begins to look dry make sure to mist with water, being careful not to oversaturate.

6. Once your seedlings emerge, place them near a sunny window or under supplemental fluorescent lights. If two seedlings emerge in one container keep the stronger looking seedling and snip the other one.

7. Before transplanting your seedlings outside permanently gradually give them time to get used to the elements outdoors. This process is called hardening off. Every day give them a few more hours outdoors before finally moving them there for good.

DEVELOPMENTAL BENEFITS:

*Handling small seeds is great for fine motor control. The process of seed starting will help children improve the dexterity of their fingers, hands, and wrist. They also enjoy touching the seeds and observing the differences in shape, size and color between the plant varieties.

Decorated Flower Pot

Flower pots can be for flowers but also for peppers, cherry tomatoes, and a wide variety of other plants. Add your own unique touch to a flower pot by decorating it before you plant. Decorated flower pots make great gifts and you can also use them in your pretend flower farm play set-up.

TIME: 45 minutes

SUPPLIES:

*Terra-cotta or other clay flower pot

*A large collection of sticks that are similar in length and about as tall as your flower pot

*Rubber band or twine

[QY0875_073]

INSTRUCTIONS:

1. Stand your sticks up around the outer edge of your pot.

2. Wrap your sticks tightly with time, looping around the outside of the pot several times.

3. Tie tightly with a bow.

4. Alternatively, you could put a large rubber band around the outside of the pot and slide your sticks underneath. Once you are finished, cover the rubber band with your twine or some pretty ribbon.

ALTERNATIVE DECORATING IDEAS:

*Use outdoor acrylic paints to paint the outside of your flower pot. You can use paintbrushes, stencils, sponges or even your nature paint brushes! The paint will dry quickly, often in just 20 minutes.

*Try painting different sized pots. Pots come as small as just a few inches.

*Washi tape or painter's tape will help you paint with straight lines. Leave blank areas that you can fill in with decor at a later time (optional).

*If your pot comes with a clay saucer, paint that too!

4.

1.

2.

Farm Harvest

Harvest time can span several months or even the entire year depending upon where you live and what types of systems you use to sow and reap. The process of seedtime to harvest is an exciting one and when harvest time arrives there is lots of reward. Harvest time also provides many learning opportunities.

TIME: 30 - 90 minutes

SUPPLIES NEEDED:

*Personal garden area or local farm

*Proper harvesting tools such as pruning shears or a garden fork

*Kid-sized harvest basket, optional

*Gardening gloves, optional

INSTRUCTIONS:

1. Determine the harvest schedule in your area. Choose something you can harvest at your home in a garden area or a container garden. As another option, consider checking at a local farm for harvest opportunities. Remember that even if you have limited space there are still gardening options such as windowsill gardening or hanging potted plants.

2. Learn about the item you are harvesting. Remember that bigger is not always better. There are several things to consider when it comes to knowing if a crop is ready to be harvested. A simple garden harvest guide book will help walk you through the knowledge you need.

3. Once you know you are ready to harvest, use the appropriate method to remove your fruit, vegetable or flower and place it in your harvest basket. If you don't have a basket you can roll up the bottom of your shirt and use that as a pouch to place your harvested items. Grown-ups may need to help here, depending upon what you are harvesting. Apples can easily be pulled from trees and blueberries are simple to snag from bushes, but thick pumpkin vines usually need to be cut with gardening shears.

Depending on the age of the child, this task may need to be done by an adult.

4. Enjoy all of the different sizes, shapes, tastes, smells, and colors you find at harvest time!

5. What will you do with your harvest? Freshly cut flowers can be used to make floral arrangements for your kitchen table or windowsill. Fruits and veggies can be washed and eaten or used to cook flavorful dishes. When children are involved with growing, preparing and cooking food, it helps improve their diet.

EASY FRUITS, VEGETABLES, AND FLOWERS TO GROW WITH KIDS: carrots, beets, potatoes, zinnias, radishes, sugar snap peas, beans, zucchini, pumpkins, sunflowers, strawberries, and cherry tomatoes.

Mud Kitchen

An outdoor pretend cooking area can provide endless entertainment for children as they cook, stir, mix, chop and create. Nature provides all the resources we need. The set-up for your mud kitchen can be elaborate or extremely simple.

TIME: 30 - 60 minutes to set up
Hours of outdoor play and creativity

SUPPLIES:

*Common kitchen items such as pots, pans, lids, cups, salt and pepper shakers, mixing bowls, whisks, wooden spoons, spatulas, muffin tins and more!

*Flat area such as a table, the top of a straw bale, or a constructed kitchen either store bought or homemade

*Dirt, water, and other natural elements such as grasses, acorns, and flowers

INSTRUCTIONS:

1. Set out your materials on your flat surface.

2. Create some mud or allow the child to create mud by combining dirt and water together.

3. Allow children to freely explore and use the materials you've provided to cook and bake all sorts of nature concoctions. Join in the fun as well with a mud cake or some stone soup.

4. Use nature's decor to give your baked goods some extra flair. Flower petals, herbs, grasses, and feathers are great items to use for chefs in the kitchen!

BENEFITS OF MUD: Dirt contains a microscopic bacteria called Mycobacterium Vaccae. This bacteria does so much for our minds, moods, and overall health. Mycobacterium Vaccae increases the levels of serotonin in our brains. Serotonin is the key hormone that helps us calm down. It stabilizes our mood and helps us feel happy and relaxed. In fact, some scientists say that exposing children to this common bacteria found in dirt and mud will help reduce their vulnerability to depression. Mycobacterium Vaccae also stimulates the immune system leading to decreased levels of childhood allergies and asthma.

4.

Supplies

3.

CHAPTER 3

OUTDOOR ARTISTS

Nature's Beauty Used to Create

A report from the Americans for the Arts concluded that children who regularly engage in artistic activities are four times more likely to be recognized for academic achievement! Art does so much for kids. It helps improve fine motor skills such as finger coordination and dexterity through cutting, glueing, drawing, and painting. Engaging in artistic endeavors also enhances creativity, augments problem-solving abilities, and helps children process their emotions.

Nature provides us with a fabulous setting to create art as well as a plethora of natural materials to use in artistic endeavors. Consider sitting amongst a field of wildflowers, a light but steady breeze blowing across your face and the sounds of birds chirping in the distance while you work on a nature painting or a nature journal entry. Utilizing nature in our art experiences increases the amount of sensory experiences children have. The more senses we engage, the more brain neurons are firing.

Within natural settings you can find beautiful color palettes, stunning symmetry, and a dazzling array of patterns. We can use nature as an inspiration for the art we create. We can use the tools of nature to create unique art experiences, both for ourselves and for our children.

Collect your interesting nature items, and get ready to create!

Nature Paint Brushes

Nature paint brushes are a wonderful way to learn about a variety of outdoor textures. See how many different types of designs you can come up with using paint brushes made entirely out of nature items. Nature art is a calming activity, great for emotional health and well-being.

TIME: 45 minutes to collect and build your brushes which will open to door to some endless artistic opportunities

[QY0872_091]

SUPPLIES:

*A variety of sticks in all shapes and sizes, small enough in length and circumference to be held by the hand

*Differently textured leaves, flowers, weeds, feathers, pine needles, spruce needles, or other natural items you find outside

*Twine or small rubber bands

*Paper or something else to paint on such as a large white sheet, cardboard, or a paper plate

*Paints

*Glass of water

INSTRUCTIONS:

1. Head outside and gather up your materials. You are looking for variety, a variety of small sticks and an assortment of leaves and flowers.

2. Using twine or small rubber bands, attach the leaves and flowers to the top of your sticks. If you are using delicate nature items, tie your twine or secure your rubber bands first and then gently slide your nature item underneath. If your item is large or has a lot of elements, like a collection of pine needles, try to distribute them evenly around the end of your nature paint brush.

3. Use your nature paint brushes to paint on a variety of surfaces. Experiment with different types of brush strokes. Try making long sweeping strokes with your paint brush and then try doing a dabbing technique. If your nature paint brush is small enough you can swish it around in a glass of water before changing paint colors. This type of art is considered process art. You aren't as concerned as much with an end product, as you are with enjoying the experience.

4. Once you are done you can give your paint brushes a quick rinse, wait for them to dry, and then use them again! Notice how the different nature textures create an abundance of variety on your painting surface.

4.

3.

2.

Flower Pressed Clay Bowls

Air-dry or self-hardening clay is a cheap, easy crafting material to use and it doesn't require an oven or a kiln to cure. This open-ended nature craft allows for all sorts of creativity and is great for working on fine motor skills. Your finished pressed bowl would be a perfect receptacle for some of your favorite nature treasures.

TIME: 30 minutes to create / 3 hours to dry

SUPPLIES:

*Bits of nature that will lay flat such as flower petals, pressed flowers, pine needles, etc.

*Self-hardening or air-dry modeling clay

*Craft glue like Mod Podge, matte or glossy finish

*Acrylic or tempera paint, optional

INSTRUCTIONS:

1. Form your modeling clay into a ball shape of your desired size. The more clay you use the larger your bowl will be.

2. Press your fingers down into the middle of the ball and continue pressing to form a bowl shape. You can also experiment with other shapes. Make your clay into a deep bowl, a shallow bowl, a cloud shaped bowl, an animal shaped plate, and so on. Try and keep your clay as smooth as possible so it will remain smooth throughout the drying process.

3. Add your favorite bits of nature to your pressed bowl by pressing them gently into the clay. You can decorate both the inside and the outside.

4. Cover your bowl on all sides with Mod Podge or other craft glue and leave it to dry for several hours.

ALTERNATIVE DECORATING IDEAS:

*Paint directly on your pressed clay bowl once it has dried completely (twenty-four to seventy-two hours depending on the thickness of your clay) but before you have applied your craft glue.

*Use rubber stamps to press into your clay bowl and then remove to make different designs. Anything textured will leave a beautiful design in your bowl. Use some of the nature items you've collected for other activities to use in this activity as well.

*Add buttons or sequins to your natural items.

*Poke a whole in the top of your clay plate with a straw and then string it with twine once it is dry. Hang your air-dry clay creations around your home or in a tree.

*Decorate your bowl with your nature glitter and use it as a fancy trinket collector.

Cardboard Nature Designs

Repurpose old cardboard boxes you have lying around into beautiful nature designs. You could shape your cardboard into any shape or design, and then by adding bits of nature, you will have a one-of-a-kind piece of art. These would work great for a party or nature school group because they are easy to set up ahead of time and offer an endless amount of possibilities to decorate.

TIME: 30 - 60 minutes

SUPPLIES:

*Cardboard, either from old cardboard boxes or cardboard sheets you have purchased

*Hole punch

*Scissors

*Tape

*Flowers with stems

INSTRUCTIONS:

1. Draw an outline of anything you would like to decorate onto your cardboard. This could be a rectangular or other shaped frame, a vase with flower stems, a wildflower field scene, a woodland animal, etc.

2. Cut out the shape you've made with scissors.

3. Using your hole punch, make holes where you would like to weave through your flowers.

4. Weave flowers through the holes you've made, taping the stems onto the backside. Experiment with different colors and patterns and see what beautiful creations you can come up with!

5. Keep your creations until the flowers dry and begin to change color. At the beginning, they will be bright and vibrant and as time wears on the colors will become more subdued.

WORKING ON FINE MOTOR CONTROL:
Fine motor control is needed for many everyday tasks such as buttoning a shirt, writing out a to-do list, and brushing hair. Any activities that children engage in that utilize small muscles in the wrists, hands, and fingers will help them in subsequent life tasks that rely on fine motor skills. Weaving flower stems into small, prepared holes helps not only with fine motor control but also with hand-eye coordination. There are so many benefits that coincide with simple nature activities!

3.

3.

Colorful Suncatcher

Almost any craft you make with pressed flowers or pressed leaves is sure to turn out beautifully. These suncatchers are an easy and rewarding craft and can be used to capture the gorgeous sunlight as it streams through the colors and textures of your flowers and leaves. If you're making nature glitter you can also use that in this project.

TIME: 45 - 60 minutes

SUPPLIES:

*Paper plate, pre-paint and let dry if you would like to.

*Contact paper or sticky back plastic

*A collection of mostly flat flowers, leaves and grasses, pressed leaves and flowers are ideal if you have any available

*Scissors

*Hole punch

*Twine

*Tweezers, optional

INSTRUCTIONS:

1. Cut out the center of the paper plate so that only a narrow border of the plate remains. Write the date along the backside of the paper plate ring so you'll remember what season you made it in.

2. Place your contact paper or sticky back plastic onto the back of the plate facing upwards so there will be a sticky circle in the middle to attach pressed flowers and leaves. Cut off any access around the edge of the paper plate.

3. Affix flowers and leaves to the sticky surface. This can be done in any manner. Flowers may overlap each other a bit or be completely separated. They can be lined up straight or scattered around.
You could even make a nature mandala design.

Remember to work carefully so as not to rip any of the delicate petals. You may want to use tweezers if you are working with pressed flowers and leaves.

4. Once you are finished, layer one last piece of contact paper over the flowers and leaves facing the opposite direction to hold it all together. Cut around the outer edge and discard any pieces you don't need.

5. Using a whole punch, punch a small hole along the ring at what you choose to be the top of your suncatcher. Thread a piece of twine through your hole, make a loop, and knot your twine.

6. Hang your suncatcher in a sunny location, swoon, and then make some more!

Homemade Nature Jewelry

Get ready to dress up and pretend with your very own homemade nature jewelry! There are so many types of jewelry you can create with the natural materials that are all around you. These also make unique homemade gifts or package decor.

TIME: 30 - 60 minutes

SUPPLIES:

*Drill and drill bits

*Walnut shells and acorn tops

*Twine

*Scissors

*Paint or paint pens, optional

INSTRUCTIONS:

1. Drill holes in your walnut shells and acorn tops that are big enough to slide a piece of twine through. Try drilling through your shells and tops at different directions and angles to add variety to your homemade jewelry. You can even drill through an acorn cap with the nut still attached. In this case, the twine will go through both the acorn cap and a small portion of nut.

2. Using your twine, string together acorns and walnuts to make necklaces, bracelets, headbands, rings, and more.

TAKE IT FURTHER: Use some of the acorn tops you painted for your memory game to add some color to your nature jewelry. Or paint your jewelry once you've strung it all together. If you strung some acorns together that have the nut part still attached, you can use paint to create faces on the nut portion similar to pinecone fairies.

TAKE IT WITH YOU: Childhood is often filled with a lot of waiting. Instead of filling waiting time with screens, bring simple materials such as these pre-drilled walnut shells and acorn tops along with some twine with you! While you are sitting in the car, waiting for an appointment, or dining at a restaurant, kids can use that time to work on some nimble fine-motor skills and enhance creativity. Some families create a "waiting place bag" filled with engaging, hands-on activities. Homemade nature jewelry would be a great addition to your waiting place bag.

2.

2.

Nature Clay Prints

You can make nature imprints onto bits of clay. This will make it easier to see the shapes and the patterns made outside. This activity can be done year round with whatever bits of nature you can find, from spring buds to seed heads at the end of harvest season. If you are in a season where you can't find many options for your clay prints, considering asking a local florist, greenhouse, or nature area if they would be willing to donate their flower scraps.

SUPPLIES:

*Small leaves, ferns, seed heads or flowers (some florists may be willing to provide their flower scraps for free)

*Self-hardening or air-dry modeling clay

*Rolling pin or water bottle with smooth sides

*Parchment paper or wax paper

*Straws or chopsticks

*String or twine, optional

*Beads and sequins, optional

*Watercolor or acrylic paint, optional

INSTRUCTIONS:

1. Take a small ball of clay and work it through your hands for about five minutes until it is soft and pliable.

2. Roll your clay into a ball and flatten it with a rolling pin on parchment or wax paper.

3. Place your leaf, flower, fern, or seed head on top of your clay and gently press it with the palm of your hand, playing close attention to the outer edges and every ridged vein.

4. Peel away whatever you used and your clay print is complete. You can use a straw or chopstick to poke a hole through the top of your print if you would like to hang it at a later time.

ALTERNATIVE DECORATING IDEAS:

*Turn your clay print into a pendant, ornament, mobile, gift embellishment, or set of wind chimes.

*Once your clay prints are completely dry you can paint them. Experiment with different types of paint such as watercolors, acrylics, or spray paint. Paint the entire print one specific color and the outer edges a different color and watch the details of your print pop before your eyes. Metal acrylic paints in gold and silver make your prints look extra fancy.

*Before your clay has dried press some beads and sequins around the edges. Make a pattern or try an unpatterned unique motif.

*Depending upon how you've decorated, if you've poked a hole in the top of your print you could use it as a holiday ornament or as an embellishment on a package.

Nature Enhanced Drawings

Little bits of nature can go a long way! Bring the colors and textures of nature to your artwork. Starting with just a simple template your creativity can soar.

TIME: 30 - 60 minutes

SUPPLIES:

*Cardboard, cardstock, or paper

*Pencil or marker

*Scissors

*Glue stick

*A small collection of nature bits such as leaves, flowers, and feathers

INSTRUCTIONS:

1. Make a template on your cardboard, cardstock or paper. Your template could be a person, an animal, a building, a forest scene or anything else that piques your interest. Leave your template minimal so there is lots room to add on bits of nature.

2. Using the natural items you've collected, glue them onto your template to enhance your design.

ART INSPIRATION: Nature has long been a source of inspiration for artists. Incorporating actual bits of nature, such as in nature enhanced drawings, is a way to blend nature and art together in a mixed-media way. Mixed media is a type of artwork that includes more than one material. In this case you are using a pencil or a marker to create a portion of your design and then natural materials to give your design some finishing touches. Artists also add materials found in nature to their paintings and sculptures. In fact, the pressed clay bowls you made are also an example of mixed media.

2.

Leaf Rubbings

Leaf rubbings are an age old activity that always capture the fascination of the child. Your paper transforms from a blank sheet to a beautiful image almost instantly, filled with swirls and patterns. As the veins emerge on the paper you can discuss how veins are vessels that carry food and water to the tree similar to how our own veins are vessels within our bodies. This quickly becomes a biology lesson!

TIME: 15 minutes

SUPPLIES:

*A variety of leaves in different shapes and sizes. Leaves can be dried or freshly fallen, just make sure they are not wet, though dry and brittle leaves may be prone to breaking.

*Tracing paper

*Different art mediums such as wax crayons, oil pastels, colored pencils and markers

*A clipboard or other hard surface

INSTRUCTIONS:

1. Secure both a leaf and your tracing paper to a clipboard, if you have one, making sure to put the leaf on the bottom. The clipboard will help keep your paper and your leaf from sliding around.

2. Slowly rub over the top of the entire leaf with your preferred art medium and watch the outline and the details of the leaf emerge. Depending on what medium you are using it will be easiest to turn it on its side for rubbing. Once you are finished, remove your leaf from behind your paper.

ALTERNATIVE DECORATING IDEAS:

*Create a layered leaf collage on one sheet of paper by doing one leaf at a time but overlapping them as you go.

*Create a leaf collage on a large sheet of butcher paper and use it as gift wrap throughout the year.

*On a single sheet of paper put a beautiful leaf rubbing near the top and use it as homemade stationary.

*Instead of leaves try rubbings with feathers, ferns, or flowers.

*Color the inside of your leaf once you have finished your leaf rubbing.

*Once you are finished with your rubbings, take a crayon or marker to outline each leaf and the veins to make those parts more prominent.

*Do a leaf rubbing on one side of a leaf and then turn the leaf over and do a different rubbing. Notice the similarities and differences between using both sides.

Mandala Designs

A mandala is a circular structure with a design that radiates symmetrically from a central point. Nature's mandalas are all around us. You can see mandala patterns in flowers petals, seashells, spiderwebs, snowflakes, tree rings and more. You can also create your own!

TIME: 30 - 90 minutes

SUPPLIES:

*An abundance of natural materials such as twigs, leaves, flowers, ferns, shells, berries, sea glass, pinecones, acorns, and grasses

*A flat surface to work on

INSTRUCTIONS:

1. Choose an item to be the center of your circular structure. You may want to choose one of your most vibrant, exciting items. Lay out your item on a flat surface such as the ground that has been cleared of debris, a flat rock, or a large wooden board.

2. Work your way out from the center laying items down in a symmetrical pattern. Mandalas can be large or small. Once you've got the process down, create another! You can even create a mandala in your color suncatcher or create a tiny mandala in your clay-pressed bowl.

MANDALAS: Now that you've made your own mandala, be on the look for these symmetrical patterns in nature. Nearly all flowers have a mandala design but some are easier to see than others. For example, a sunflower bud, a petunia and a zinnia all have a unique center with a symmetrical design that radiates out through the petals. A conch shell comes to a point right in the middle and then spirals out in a symmetrical pattern. A cross-slice of a lemon cucumber looks like a flower and is another example of a nature mandala. Even the human eye has this pattern. Look around you and see what other natural mandalas you can find in the world!

Supplies

2.

CHAPTER 4

NATURE COLLECTORS

Nature's Bounty Ready to Find

Nature is teaming with possibility! It is jam-packed with what are often referred to as "loose parts". Loose parts are any types of materials that have no defined use. During play, the child incorporates his or her imagination, taking the materials available and transforming them into something entirely made up. When items have no defined use, there is an endless amount of options for play.

Sticks can become magic wands, trucks, baby dolls, or spaghetti. Rocks can make plates for fairies or be used to build a dam in a small creek. Nature doesn't skimp on quantity. Inside toys are often fought over because there may be only one type of stuffed animal or one type of action figure. Outside, natural materials abound and there is almost always extra. Kids can find an endless supply of things to play with and to share.

Natural materials feel good to the touch. If allowed, it can be fun to collect little bits of nature treasure on your outings. Smooth stones feel so good when hands go in pockets. Nature shelves filled with feathers, pebbles and shells can bring back memories from outside adventures. Natural materials can also be used for all sorts of adored crafts and activities.

When we use nature's toys, there are no batteries needed! Every bit of nature runs on the creativity of the child.

Nature Bracelet

Keep a little tape on hand in your backpack or even in your first aid kit. This activity will always be ready to go! This simple craft will entice kids to find a variety of nature elements outside. They can stick their findings to their bracelets in a random fashion or make a pattern.

TIME: 15 minutes

SUPPLIES:

*Masking tape or duct tape, enough to wrap loosely around the wrist

*Bit of nature that you have collected in the past or that you find along your outdoor journey

*Scissors, optional

INSTRUCTIONS:

1. Place a piece of tape loosely around the wrist with the sticky side facing out. Cut or rip the tape in a straight line and attach one side to the other to form a bracelet.

2. Head out for a walk and stick some of the things you find to your sticky bracelet. It's that simple! The colors and textures of the items you find will make a beautiful bracelet. Look for pinecones, seeds, grasses, leaves, and flowers. You can keep adding elements until there is no room left or you can leave a little space for different designs. This activity helps children become more observant about the world around them.

3. This activity could also be done with bits of nature you have already collected such as pressed flowers or your nature glitter.

WATCH OUT: Be sure to familiarize yourself with poison ivy and poison oak before beginning this activity. Poison ivy has three leaves that are shiny with smooth or slightly notched edges. Poison oak has larger leaves that have a textured, hairy surface.

TAKE IT FURTHER: There are all sorts of ways to add some variation to this craft such as searching for items of a certain color or even trying to spell a name or another word with your natural finds! Talk about all the things you found that you couldn't affix to a bracelet such as insects or large items.

2.

2.

3.

Wax Dipped Leaves

Dipping leaves in wax helps preserve their vibrant color. You can do this any time of the year. If you live in an area where the leaves look like fire just before they drop, go collect some and dip them in wax and bottle up the season. Once your leaves are cool you can use these for all sorts of decor and play!

TIME: 30 - 60 minutes

SUPPLIES:

*Leaves of different shapes, sizes, and colors

*Beeswax in pellet form or cut into small bits, paraffin wax, or the nubs of old candles

*Double broiler or small slow-cooker

*Wax paper

INSTRUCTIONS:

1. Slowly melt your wax. Be careful not to let it boil. You can do this in a double boiler or in a crockpot. It will take about thirty minutes for the wax to melt inside of a slow-cooker. Dried wax can be removed but it is difficult so take this into account. If you'd like, you can wrap whatever you are melting your wax in with aluminum foil.

2. Dip your leaves into the wax until the flat parts of the leaf (called the blades) are completely covered, one at a time, holding onto the stem. You can also do this by very carefully pouring your melted wax into a rimmed sheet-pan that is lined with aluminum foil and then dipping your leaves into the shallow layer of wax that is in the pan.

3. Gently shake off any excess wax so it doesn't clump up and lay your leaves flat to dry on wax paper. Alternatively, you could hang them with clothespins above wax paper or something else that would catch any drips. Wax dipped leaves dry quickly.

4. Repeat with a second coat if desired. The more coats of wax you apply, the more you will be able to see the wax.

TAKE IT FURTHER: Wax dipped leaves make beautiful garlands, mobiles, and even leaf crowns. Glue them on top of pumpkins or watermelons to create a whimsical fairy house.

Why do leaves change color? During the long ,warm days of the year, leaves convert energy from the sun into food for the trees they are connected to. Chlorophyll is the chemical in the leaf that allows it to create the sugars and starches from sunlight that the tree uses for food. Chlorophyll is what gives the leaf its green color. As the days grow shorter and colder, the leaves stop creating food and trees begin preparing for winter. With all the chlorophyll gone, the green color starts to fade and we can see the other pigments of the leaves. For a short period of time, until the leaves fall to the ground, we experience the vibrant red, orange, yellow and even purple colors of the changing leaves.

Nature Glitter

Eco-friendly nature glitter that can also be used as table decor, confetti and so much more! Kids love to make this colorful glitter and it gives their fine motor skills a little boost. Since hole punches come in all shapes and sizes you can adapt this activity to the season to make it even more festive.

TIME: 20 - 30 minutes

SUPPLIES:
*A variety of leaves
*A hole punch or several different hole punches that punch out different shapes

INSTRUCTIONS:
1. Collect some leaves. Try and find variety in color, if you can. You can even use your wax-dipped leaves from this year or from years past.

2. Use a circular hole punch or hole punches with different shapes to punch holes in the leaves and then collect the cut pieces in a container. You can buy hole punches in the shapes of stars, hearts, leaves, flowers, trees, and even teddy bears! With the large variety of hole punch shapes available you could make dedicated nature glitter for many different seasons and celebrations.

3. Keep your cut pieces in the fridge to help the color last a little bit longer. Cut pieces stored in the fridge will retain their luster for about one week.

TAKE IT FURTHER: Use your glitter for some of the other projects in this book like the flower pressed pinched clay bowls, color suncatchers, nature bracelets, and nature mandalas. Store your glitter in pretty vials and keep them on hand for when you're playing in your mud kitchen. Be on the lookout for unique vials at garage sales, flea markets, or antique stores.

2.

PUMPKIN
VILLAGE

3.

Pumpkin Fairy Village

Time: 60-90 min

I've spent my whole life carving pumpkins with faces. It's just as easy, if not easier, to add some doors and windows to pumpkins. Turn them into little houses to play with. Let your creativity soar with a new twist on pumpkin carving. If you have several pumpkins on hand you can turn your pumpkin houses into a small village.

TIME: 60 - 90 minutes

SUPPLIES:

*A pumpkin or a variety of pumpkins in all sorts of shapes, sizes and colors. Look for pumpkins with flat bottoms so they won't fall over or roll away.

*Carving knife

*Ice cream scoop or spoon

*Permanent marker

*Pencil

*Paper

*Small bits of nature like twigs or corn stalks, optional

*Heated glue dispenser, optional

*Glue sticks for heated glue dispenser, optional

*Craft paint, optional

*Paintbrush, optional

*Wax-dipped leaves, optional

*Toothpicks, optional

INSTRUCTIONS:

1. Cut out your pumpkin lid by carving around the top of the pumpkin in a circular shape but on an angle so the lid won't fall through the hole opening when your pumpkin is finished.

2. Scoop out all of the pulp from the inside of the pumpkin making sure to scrape and clear the sides. There are special types of scoopers you can get for this job or you can use a regular kitchen spoon or ice cream scooper.

3. Sketch out your pumpkin house design on paper, considering where the light comes through. Rounded doors and windows often have a magical touch.

4. Transfer your design to your pumpkin and carve out your shapes.

5. Use some of the pieces of your carved pumpkin that you've pulled out, and any other bits of nature that you have on hand, to add some finishing touches to your pumpkin house. You could make a chimney, add small pieces of twigs for window frames, or use your wax-dipped leaves to make a beautiful roof. Heated glue is an option to use for this step. For some elements a simple toothpick will work to hold everything together.

TAKE IT FURTHER: Set up an entire pumpkin village. You can use this as a grand display or as a play area for children. Use what you have on hand to make elevation changes and roads. Decorate with some of the other projects you've made like your twig stars. The base of your stick raft might make a great bridge or a walkway. There are endless opportunities for creativity in your pumpkin village! Don't forget to light it up at night.

Wildflower Playdough

Manipulating play-dough helps children build strong muscles in their fingers and hands. As children roll, pound, twist, pinch and knead the dough they will be developing many skills all while having fun. Adding wildflowers to homemade playdough adds extra sensory elements through new textures, smells and colors.

TIME: 20 minutes to make the dough, endless amounts of playdough play

SUPPLIES:

*1 cup flour (236.6 ml)

*⅓ cup salt (78.9 ml)

*1 - 2 TBS vegetable oil (14.8 - 29.6 ml)

*1 cup boiling water (236.6 ml)

*1 cup chopped wildflowers (236.6 ml)

*Food coloring, optional

*Essential oils, optional

INSTRUCTIONS:

1. Grab a small basket or a bag and head out on a hunt for wildflowers! Wildflowers come in all shapes and sizes and you don't need many. Just one cup will help you create a beautiful batch of playdough that has a unique color and texture. Consider collecting other nature items you could either add to the dough or use to create art with the finished play-dough.

2. Combine and mix the dry ingredients in a bowl.

3. Blend boiling water and chopped wildflowers in a blender. Add a few drops of food coloring and essential oils at this step if you are using these items.

4. Add wet ingredients to dry ingredients and stir.

5. Add oil to desired consistency.

6. Let the dough cool. Store in an air-tight container when not in use

TAKE IT FURTHER: What other nature elements could you add to playdough? How about cut-up leaves or finely chopped pine needles? Some blades of grass? What ideas do you have? What natural elements could you use to mold and play with the dough? Pinecones? Acorns? Sticks? What happens when you mix colors? Which colors are your favorite? What does your playdough smell like? What natural items might give it a different smell? Can you make dough in a rainbow of colors?

1.

3.

3.

Memory Game

This is a different take on the classic memory game, designed to help stretch the child's brain! The added bonus is that making and playing this game will help improve fine motor skills. Depending upon what natural materials you use, this game can easily be kept on hand in a diaper bag or purse to play whenever and wherever you have a quick moment.

TIME: 15 minutes to create
24 hours to dry
10 minute to play

SUPPLIES:

*An even number of acorn tops

*Several different colors of acrylic paint

*Paintbrushes

INSTRUCTIONS:

1. Paint the underside of your acorn tops, making sure that each top will have one other acorn top with a matching color.

2. Let your acorn tops dry.

HOW TO PLAY:

1. Place all of your acorn tops colored side down.

2. Choose a player to start first.

3. The first player picks up and looks at the underside of two acorn tops, allowing every player to see the colors.

4. If the colors are a match, the player gets to keep those acorn tops and go again. If the colors are not a match, the player must return the acorn tops to their original location and the next player gets to go.

5. Play until all acorn tops have been matched up. At the end, the winner is the player who has found the most matches!

VARIATIONS: There are so many variations you could do with this game. You could use seashells or the bottoms of leaves. Instead of paint brushes you could use paint pens or markers depending upon the type of surface you are working with. Colors are fun to match but you could use this as an activity to learn shapes or match up lowercase with uppercase letters. The sky's the limit here!

Flower Pounding (Hapa Zome)

Hapa Zome is Japanese for "leaf dye". This activity will take you through the process of transferring the natural pigments from leaves or flowers onto paper or fabric to create a color image. Within just a few seconds of hammering, you'll have a beautiful nature design.

TIME: 15 - 20 minutes

SUPPLIES:

*White cloth fabric or white paper

*A hammer, a rubber mallet, or a rock

*An assortment of brightly colored flowers and leaves that aren't dried out, such as nasturtium flowers (really easy to grow), pansies, tomato leaves, poppy petals, geraniums, ferns, and autumn leaves

INSTRUCTIONS:

1. Place your paper or fabric on a hard surface such as a table, clipboard, cutting board, or large wood circle.

2. Arrange your flowers and leaves on your fabric or paper and then cover with another piece of fabric or another piece of paper. You can leave the flowers hole or break off petals to create interesting patterns.

3. Tap all over your top layer with whatever tool you have on hand. Be extra careful if you are using paper not to rip it. You will start to see the color come through. Experiment with different amounts of pressure. Determine how firmly you need to tap to obtain the desired effect. Most flowers require steady, firm taps but some leaves with less moisture in them may need more of a whack.

4. Take off your top layer and view your creation! Peel off any remaining foliage and your entire design will be revealed. At this point you can add more if you'd like.

5. If you used fabric you can iron your final design image in order to help set the colors and prevent them from fading.

ALTERNATIVE DECORATING IDEAS:

*Create your designs on large sheets of paper and when everything has dried you can use your decorated paper as wrapping paper.

*Cut your finished designs into rectangles and use them as bookmarks.

*Connect your designs with twine or yarn and create a bunting, a festive decoration made of fabric or paper. What a great addition to your forest teepee!

2.

3.

Pinecone Fairies

Pinecone creatures make adorable ornaments and play things. Beyond fairies you can make all sorts of animals like owls, mice, and penguins. By simply adding a piece of ribbon, these turn into adorable ornaments.

TIME: 20 - 60 minutes

SUPPLIES:

*Pinecones, experiment with different shapes and sizes

*Acron with cap

*Heated glue dispenser

*Glue sticks for heated glue dispenser

*Craft paint

*Paintbrush

*Paint pens

*Nature items for accessories such as flower petals and feathers

*Twinc or ribbon, optional

INSTRUCTIONS:

1. Paint your pinecone. This will be the fairy's body. It is a fun process to try and paint every nook and cranny of the pinecone. You can paint it all one color or make it a mix of colors.There are twenty different varieties of pine cone so depending on which type you choose or which type you have available near where you live, your pinecone fairies can come in a variety of shapes and sizes.

2. Paint the acorn. The top of the acorn that tends to be rough and scaly often resembles a hat is called the cupule. Paint the cupule to look like your fairy's hat.

Turn the main acorn shell into your fairy's hair and face using paint and paint pens. You can paint hair coming from out of the cupule and sweeping to the sides and around the back. Then use your paint pens to add a face.

3. Add embellishments like flower petals or feathers to your fairy using a heated glue dispenser. Allow your fairy to dry completely before playing with it.

DID YOU KNOW? The largest type of pine cone comes from the coulter pine tree, native to South California and Mexico. Pine cones from the coulter pine tree can weigh up to eleven pounds (five kg). The longest pine cones come from sugar pine and can grow to 24 inches (61 cm) in length!

Sun Prints

Grab a pack of cyanotype paper and let the creativity begin! This type of paper is light-sensitized and when it is exposed to sunlight an image is produced in just a few minutes. Using this type of paper is an excellent introduction into the photographic process, because light will create an image on paper the same way it would create an image in a camera.

TIME: 15 - 20 minutes

SUPPLIES:

*Cyanotype paper

*A piece of cardboard bigger than the paper

*Push pins, optional

*A small piece of plexiglass to lay on top of nature objects, optional

*Nature specimens of different shapes and sizes [QY0872_155]

INSTRUCTIONS:

1. Place your cyanotype paper with the blue side facing up on a piece of cardboard. To keep your paper for sliding around, pin the corners to the piece of cardboard with pushpins.

2.In a shady area or back inside, select flat objects from your nature collection that have an interesting shape and lay them on your cyanotype paper, making sure to keep the blue side facing up. You can lay singular objects or use several objects to make designs. This is a fabulous outlet for creativity.

3. Once you are satisfied with your creation, expose your cyanotype paper to direct sunlight for two to five minutes. Do not over expose. You will see the blue of your paper begin to fade to a very light blue, almost white. On a cloudy day, the time could take up to thirty minutes. If it is a windy day and your objects are light, you can lay a piece of plexiglass on top of them to keep them from blowing in the breeze. You'll want your objects to stay perfectly still for the entire two minute exposure to sunlight.

4. Remove your objects from the paper, step out of the direct sunlight, and rinse your sunprint in water to wash off the chemicals. You need to actually rinse your paper instead of just submerging it in water. During the rinsing process, you are rinsing away the blue molecules that are sensitive to ultra-violet light that were embedded in the cyanotype paper. Immediately the white parts of your paper will turn dark blue and your shapes will turn white. It is a fascinating process to watch.

5. Hang or lay flat to dry. The edges have a tendency to curl up so if you want your finished product to stay flat, place it on a level surface and put something heavy like a book on top of it until it dries completely.

Supplies

2.

CHAPTER 5

CRITTER ADMIRERS

Nature's Creatures Captivate All Audiences

Common wild creatures such as squirrels, chipmunks, birds, ducks, snakes and frogs can be riveting to children. Wildlife opens up a whole world of wonder. There are so many things we can learn from the animals around us.

There is so much to observe when it comes to outdoor animals. The immense variety allows children to see and hear all sorts of different types of movements and animal behaviors. Certain animals are active during the day, while others are active at night. Each unique species provides a plethora of learning opportunities.

The activities in this section will provide new and interesting ways to interact with the wildlife that lives right around your home. No matter where we live, we share our world with animals.

Enjoying the wildlife that is all around you is a hobby you can enjoy for a lifetime. Start today!

Birdseed Ornaments

Children love to make these ornaments and hang them up year round as a restaurant for neighborhood birds. Hang them up and watch your feathered friends fly in to enjoy these tasty treats. Throughout the process, you can learn all sorts of new things about the types of birds that live in your geographic area.

TIME: 20 minutes to make
20 minutes to harden

SUPPLIES:
*2 cups (473 ml) of birdseed
*1 pack of unflavored gelatin
*⅓ cup (79 ml) boiling water
*2 tbsp. (30 ml) cold water
*Cookie cutters or muffin tins for the molds
*Twine
*Scissors
*Parchment paper
*Non-stick cooking spray or coconut oil
*Wooden skewer or metal straw
*Rubber scraper, optional

INSTRUCTIONS:
1. Spray the inside of your cookie cutters or muffin tin molds with non-stick cooking spray. You could also coat them in coconut oil. Either option will make your bird seed ornaments easier to pop out in the end. If you are using cookie cutters lay them on a piece of parchment paper.

2. Mix together one package of unflavored gelatin with two tablespoons (30 ml) of cold water and let your mixture sit for one minute.

3. Add ⅓ cup (79 ml) of boiling water to your gelatin mixture, stirring for several minutes until the gelatin is dissolved. This mixture is what will help the bird seed stick together.

4. Pour two cups (473 ml) of bird seed into your gelatin mix and stir until it has been thoroughly mixed.

5. Carefully spoon your mixture into your cookie cutters or muffin tins and press firmly using your hands if the mixture has cooled enough or a rubber scraper.

6. Make a small hole in each cookie with a skewer or a metal straw. This is where your string will go so that you can hang your bird seed ornaments up in trees or on poles.

7. Allow your ornaments to harden. This will happen a little faster if you place them in the refrigerator for a few hours.

8. Carefully remove your birdseed ornaments from the cookie cutters or remove them from the muffin tins.

9. String a piece of twine through the hole and tie to create a loop.

10. Hang your ornaments outside and enjoy watching for birds to arrive!

TRY THIS: Skip the twine and make "bird cookies" instead. You can hide bird cookies around your yard or neighborhood and see if the birds or the squirrels find them first! Alternatively, you can hollow out oranges, apples, and even small pumpkins and fill those with bird seed to string up in trees or on poles or outdoor hooks.

DID YOU KNOW? The seed that attracts the most types of birds is the sunflower seed.

8.

10.

1.

2.

Animal Tracking

Tracking animals allows you to get a better sense of their daily lives and habits. It's fun to dream about where they might have come from and where they are going. Animal tracking can be done year-round but it's easiest to see the tracks in the mud or the snow. So head out after a good rainfall or snowfall and see what you can find!

TIME: 30 - 60 minutes of outdoor exploring

SUPPLIES:

*Animal tracking identification information, optional - you can find this information in a book such as a field guide or through different apps on your smartphone

*Magnifying glass, optional

*Nature journal and pencil, optional

INSTRUCTIONS:

1. Find an area where the tracks of animals may have left some good imprints. A thin layer of freshly fallen snow, sand, mud, or damp soil all provide places where you might come across some animal prints.

2. If you find some tracks one of the first things you can do is identify how many toes the animal has. This will help you in determining which animal left the prints.

3. Use the resources you have on hand to try and match the tracks you have found with the animal that might have made the tracks.

4. Look at the surroundings near the animal tracks and see if you can find any other clues about what the animal may have been doing. Was it traveling for water or food? Was it escaping a predator? Broken twigs, claw scratches on bark, and scat are all things that can give you clues about an animal's behavior.

STAY SAFE: Remember to never go close to a wild animal even if it tries to approach you or appears to be friendly.

BEFORE YOU GO: Learn about what animals are native to your area so you know ahead of time which types of prints you might see while you are tracking. In the canine species, you might see dog, coyote, wolf, or fox prints. You'll know if it's part of the canine species if you see nail markings. Felines retract their claws so the prints of cats, mountain lions, bobcats, and lynxes show no nail markings. Other small mammal tracks you may come across are rabbits, mice, skunks, opossums, otters, beavers, porcupines, armadillos, wolverines, squirrels, or chipmunks. Hooved animals like deer leave distinct looking prints. Keep your eyes peeled for elk, buffalo, horse, sheep, or wild hog prints. You may come across bird prints from ducks, wild turkeys, crows, herons or eagles. And finally, depending upon where you live, you may get to see alligator or bear prints.

Bird Calls

Do you have a budding ornithologist in your home? There are so many things you can learn through the study of bird calls. Bird songs are often used for mating, for territory ownership, and for communicating about food or predators. It is fascinating to match birds with their songs.

TIME: 30 - 90 minutes

SUPPLIES:

*Binoculars, optional

*Nature journal and pencil, optional

INSTRUCTIONS:

1. Head outside, close your eyes, and listen for bird sounds. Once you've been able to distinguish the bird songs from other surrounding noises, see if you can spot the birds that are making the different songs. Use binoculars if necessary.

2. Make note of the different sounds you hear. Try and concentrate on just one bird at a time. Listen for variations in rhythm, tone, pitch and repetition. Does the song sound high-pitched or low-pitched? Melodic or harsh? Can you relate a certain song with a certain word or phrase in order to remember it better? For example, the Carolina Wren has a song that sounds like "tea-kettle," the Tufted Titmouse says, "Peter, Peter, Peter," the Red-Winged Black Bird says "conk-la-ree", and the Barred Owl asks, "Who cooks for you?"

3. Start small with trying to identify three or four varieties of birds and then expand your knowledge from there. Birding is a fantastic learning opportunity to add to your vacation experiences. As you travel to different parts of your country, or of the world, pay attention to the different bird songs you hear.

TAKE IT FURTHER:

Using an observation journal, record your experiences with listening for bird calls. Do birds tend to sing more during the morning, afternoon or evening? Are there certain months or seasons when birds seem to be the loudest? Once you start listening for birds, you may never stop listening for birds!

FORMING A BIRD CLUB:

Taking children outside to observe is one sure-fire way to increase their interest in science. Consider forming a bird club where you meet on a regular basis to participate in bird counts, to notice different bird behaviors, and to match birds with their songs. One fun activity is to count how many birds you see in a certain number of minutes. You can also join up with a club that already exists like an Audubon chapter, to learn from those who have already been birding for many years.

1.

7.

8.

Monarch Life Cycle

Time:
30-60 min

It is enthralling to watch a monarch caterpillar grow 2,000 times bigger, shed it's skin and form a brilliant green chrysalis, and finally emerge as a brilliant orange and black butterfly - all in the course of just a few weeks. There is so much to learn through the entire metamorphosis process.

TIME: 30 - 60 minutes to find and collect monarch eggs or caterpillars
About one month from egg to hatching

SUPPLIES:

*Daily fresh milkweed

*Plastic cup or container with a lid that has holes

*Mesh butterfly enclosure

*Newspaper, optional

INSTRUCTIONS:

1. Find a patch of milkweed or order a monarch caterpillar kit. Milkweed can be found in meadows, wildflower fields, prairies, and right along the side of the road. When you crack open the leaves there is a sticky, milky-looking substance inside.

2. Female butterflies lay their eggs on the underside of the milkweed leaf.

3. Place your milkweed leaf, with either your egg or caterpillar, inside of a clean plastic container. Make sure your container has a lid with holes. If your leaf has an egg on it, place the leaf egg-side up inside your container. You can place a wet paper towel below the leaf to make sure it doesn't dry out.

4. Monarch eggs will hatch within three to four days. Once the caterpillar hatches, it will eat its own eggshell and immediately begin feasting on milkweed.

5. Every day check on your egg or caterpillar. You will need to add fresh milkweed daily as well as clean out your container. Caterpillars eat a lot and produce a lot of waste. When you clean out your container, leave the caterpillar on its leaf and set it in another secure location.

6. It takes approximately two weeks for a caterpillar to start to form a chrysalis. By this point, the caterpillar will have shed its skin around five times and will be about two inches (5 cm) long. On its own, the caterpillar will move to the top of the container, hang upside down in the shape of the letter "J", shed its final skin in a twisting motion, and form a beautiful green chrysalis with gold flecks. This is called the pupa stage and it lasts anywhere from ten to fifteen days.

7. The day before the butterfly emerges, the chrysalis will turn translucent and you will be able to see the wings through the chrysalis.

8. Once the butterfly emerges it will spend several hours hanging vertically and drying out its wings. This takes three to four hours and during this period the butterfly must be left alone. Place it in a netted enclosure because once it is ready it will begin to fly! It is best to wait about 24 hours before releasing your monarch outside to give it time to mature all of its systems. Place fresh-cut flowers or fresh fruit in your enclosure while waiting for release. Before releasing, it is fun to determine if your monarch is a male or female. Males have thinner veins and a black spot on each hindwing. Females have thicker veins and no spots on their hindwings.

ACADEMIC BENEFITS: There are so many new vocabulary words to learn while raising monarchs. Caterpillar droppings are called "frass." The caterpillar moves through four stages of metamorphosis: egg, larva (caterpillar), pupa (chrysalis), and adult (butterfly). Chrysalis is a word specific to butterflies, while cocoons are made by moths.

Insect Hotel

Insect hotels offer a sanctuary to insects and they are fun to create! You can buy an insect hotel at the store but it can be more fun to make one yourself. Your hotel just might be what the insects in your area need to hibernate during the cold months.

TIME: 60 minutes

SUPPLIES:

*Some large recycled materials that are toxin-free such as wooden pallets, bricks, or old planter pots

*A large collection of natural materials such as dry leaves, pine cones, bark, twigs, straw, hay, wood chips, and bamboo

INSTRUCTIONS:

1. Choose a spot for your insect home taking care to consider what types of insects you are trying to attract. Some insects like cool and moist conditions and would prefer a shady spot while other insects prefer to be in a dry spot with full sun.

2. Create your insect hotel structure. This can be as simple as laying pallets on top of each other and using the open spaces between the wood slats or creating a structure out of rot resistant wood. You can also use items you already have on hand that have spaces that could be filled in, such as an old planter pot. Make sure your structure is secure and will not wobble or topple over.

3. Fill in the gaps of your structure with your nature materials. There are no rules here. Children love this task and often daydream about which items the insects might use as a bed.

DID YOU KNOW?

Most of your backyard bugs are beneficial. An average backyard will often have thousands of insects and 90% of those insects are either beneficial or harmless. Beneficial bugs fall into three categories: pollinators, predators, and parastizers. Pollinators allow plants to become fertilized and eventually produce fruits, seeds, or young plants. Bees, butterflies, and moths are examples of pollinators. Predators eat unwanted yard and garden pests. For example, ladybugs can eat up to forty aphids an hour. Parasitizers lay their eggs on or in the bodies of other insects. One example of this is the braconid female wasp that lays her eggs under the skin of a hornworm.

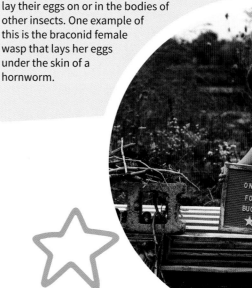

ONLY
FOR
BUGS

3.

ONLY
FOR
BUGS

3.

Seasonal Farm Visit

A seasonal visit to a farm can offer a relaxing escape from daily life. Farm life changes with the seasons so make your farm visit an annual occasion or visit each season to see transformations throughout the year. With all the variety from farm to farm, animal to animal, and season to season, the learning opportunities abound at local small farms.

TIME: One to three hours (or more!)

SUPPLIES NEEDED:
*Local farm to visit

INSTRUCTIONS:
1. Search the internet, social media, and ask around to find some local farms that are within traveling distance of your home. Many farms offer classes, exhibits, and other attractions that can provide hours of entertainment for your family. Even if you have to travel quite a ways to visit a farm, you may get a day's worth of activities out of your excursion.

2. Upon arrival find out what the farm offers that season. Maybe you will be able to pick your own produce, visit with some baby animals, watch cows being milked, or enjoy a horse-drawn wagon ride. Perhaps the farm offers a tour you can join in on. Be sure to ask lots of questions! There are so many things to learn on a farm.

3. Inquire about other seasons on that particular farm. Not every farm is open year round but some may offer several seasons worth of activities to enjoy.

WHAT IS AGRITAINMENT? Agritainment is agricultural based entertainment and it's one of our absolute favorite ways to get outside. When we head to local farms to engage in things like u-pick produce, petting and feeding animals, corn mazes, pumpkin patches, and cooking classes we learn all sorts of new things, while also getting in a lot of our outside hours for the year. Even within a small geographical region there will be all sorts of variety from farm to farm. Additionally, local farms that are open for longer than one season, offer us a sneak peak into what farm life is like year round.

Bird House

Turn your ordinary milk carton into a designer home for your favorite feathered friends. You only need a few supplies to make this one! These are simple to create and would make a great party activity.

TIME: 45 - 60 minutes

SUPPLIES:

*Rectangular milk or juice carton

*Scissors or utility knife

*Rope, twine or string

*Craft paint

*15 wooden craft sticks

*Heated glue dispenser

*Glue sticks for heated glue dispenser

*Spray paint, optional

*Paintbrushes

*Stick for the perch

INSTRUCTIONS:

1. Thoroughly wash and dry your rectangular carton with soap and warm water. Rinse, wash and dry the cap as well, making sure to keep the cap.

2. Cut a circular door in the front of your carton using scissors or an exacto knife. The hole will allow birds to fly in and out of your bird house.

3. Cut a small hole right beneath the front door that is the right size to insert your stick. The stick will act as a perch for the birds.

4. Poke a few small holes in the bottom of your carton in order to provide extra ventilation and to allow water to drain out.

5. Give your carton a base coat of paint and allow to dry. You could do this with your craft paint or with a can of spray paint. Depending on the color of your paint, you may want two base coats to begin with. This will conceal any writing or logos that were originally on the carton.

6. Add your craft stick roof. Glue two craft sticks on either side of the very top of your carton. Put a line of heated glue down the top of those craft sticks and lay your craft sticks individually along the glue line. On the top of the one side of your slanted roof, put one last line of glue, and then attach craft sticks to form the other side of your roof.

7. Decorate your milk carton with your paints! You may paint the roof if you like.

8. Cut two small holes near the top of your carton, to run your string or rope through.

9. Choose a quiet spot to hang your birdhouse, either from a tree branch, eave or other sturdy fixture. Sit back and admire your new feathered friends.

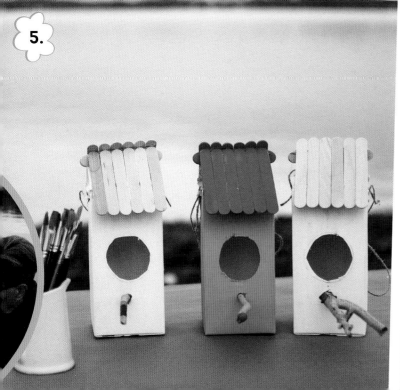

2.

3.

Squirrel Picnic Table

A pint-sized picnic table for squirrels? Yes, please! Squirrel picnic tables are easy to build and delightful to watch. You can affix them to a tree or fence post near a window or you can bring them along with you on a hike to set along a trail edge and watch and observe.

TIME: 60 - 90 minutes

SUPPLIES:

*Saw

*Nail gun and nails, wood screws and a drill, or wood glue

*5 wooden pieces that measure 2" x 8" x ¾", two for the benches and three for the tabletop

*4 wooden pieces that measure 1.5" x 5" by ¾" that are cut at a 22.5o angle

*2 seat support pieces that measure 1.5" x 12" by ¾"

*2 tabletop support pieces that measure ¾" by ¾" by 5"

*Wooden attachment piece that measures 2" x 8" x ¾" cut on one side at a 22.5o angle, optional

*Small plastic bowl with lid, optional

INSTRUCTIONS:
1. Make all of your wood cuts for your picnic table and sand your final pieces.

2. Create the sides of your squirrel picnic table by attaching one seat support and one table top support to the angled legs as shown. You can attach your pieces using a nail gun with nails, a drill with wood screws, or wood glue.

3. Stand up the sides of your picnic table and attach the two picnic table benches, as well as the three wooden pieces that make up the table top. Once again, a nail gun with nails, a drill with wood screws or wood glue would suffice.

4. Using your preferred method, attach a plastic bowl to the top of your picnic table as an optional step.

5. If you are hanging your squirrel picnic table onto a tree trunk or a fence post, affix the wooden attachment piece to one side of your picture table using a nail, screw, or wood glue. Choose a stainless steel or any other rust-proof nail or screw to attach your picnic table to a tree or fence post. Avoid putting a nail or screw into a weak or damaged tree.

6. Put food in your bowl for the squirrels and chipmunks to find, or just lay the food on the top of the picnic table. Choose from a variety of nuts, sunflower seed, fresh cut fruit or corn cobs. At first the animals may quickly grab the food and run away, but in time they may stay and dine at their very own picnic table.

PUDDLE STOMPERS

Nature's Simplicity in Water, Ice and Snow

When children splash in puddles, when they smash ice into small chunks and when they form snowballs they are doing grand experimentation. Children are naturally inclined toward the things in nature that are helpful for their development, and water elements are readily available!

No matter the time of year, nature freely provides water, ice and snow. These elements allow for all sorts of creative and enthralling play opportunities. Through sensory feedback, children are answering question after question as they learn about force, buoyancy, cause and effect and so much more.

While we may not immediately think of water, ice and snow as toys, they can be combined and manipulated in all sorts of creative ways that will provide endless hours of hands-on learning opportunities for kids. Additionally, this type of play is almost always free or nearly free as long as you can find some puddles or a water source.

In its simplicity, water in all of its forms offers so much to children.

Ice Globe

What do you get when you put a tea light inside an ice globe on a dark night? Pure magic. This activity is a must-do!

TIME: 5 minutes of active time
24 hours to freeze

SUPPLIES:

*Balloons, the size of your balloon will determine the size of your globe

*Plastic plate or tray

*Tealight, choose a battery-powered option if you want to be able to hold the ice globe

*Alternatively, you can buy an ice ball mold kit if you are avoiding the use of plastic

INSTRUCTIONS:

1. Fill a balloon with water and tie the end.

2. Set the balloon on a plastic plate, tie side up, and give it twenty-four hours to freeze completely. Depending upon climate and season, you could do this outside or use your freezer. The plastic plate will keep the bottom of the balloon from freezing through.

3. Cut off the balloon with a pair of scissors, be careful to dispose of it properly.

4. Lift the balloon off of the plate and let the remaining water inside the bottom of the globe drain out.

5. Once it is dark, place the ice globe over a tea light and experience the wonder. If you've used a battery powered tea light, you can hold your glowing ice globe in your hands.

MAKE IT EVEN MORE MAGICAL:

*Fill your globe with bits and pieces of nature like flower petals or small berries.

*Make several ice globes and light a nighttime path with them.

*Create an ice pillar with a PVC pipe and freeze your globe to the top of the pillar using a spray bottle and water on a cold night.

*Make ice globes in other shapes. Instead of using a balloon, use a small plastic container. You can fill the container with water and other nature items. Once frozen, dig out an area at the bottom just large enough to set your tea light on.

Snow Painting

Turn snow from brilliant white into a rainbow of colors! This activity combines a love of painting, with a love of color and a love of snow. Using items you have on hand, kids will be delighted with the endless artistic opportunities a little bit of snow will provide.

TIME: 10 minutes to set-up
An hour or more of art time

SUPPLIES:

*Cold water (hot or even luke-warm water could melt the snow)

*Non-toxic food coloring or home-made food coloring with foods like strawberries, raspberries, beets, carrots, blueberries, or turmeric.

*Paintbrushes

*Jars

*Squeeze bottles or spray bottles, optional

INSTRUCTIONS: [QY0872_163]
1. Fill your bottles, jars or spray bottles with cold water and a few drops of food coloring. You could keep it simple with the primary colors or you could start off with a wide variety of colors to choose from.

2. Give the children their paint brushes and colored water and allow them to paint the snow. Encourage them to combine colors and see what happens. Kids may do abstract painting or they may try and create simple images right in the snow.

3. Try making different sculptures out of snow and then painting those. There are many different artistic avenues you can take with snow and food coloring.

TAKE IT FURTHER:
Bring this activity inside! Snow painting can be done inside as well with a large bowl of snow (or even a bathtub filled with snow). Use the same supplies as above and enjoy snow painting as an indoor or outdoor creative activity.

DID YOU KNOW?
Snowflakes are formed when water vapor freezes around a dust particle or pollen in the sky. This process creates an ice crystal. Some snowflakes are made up of up to 200 ice crystals that have fused together while other snowflakes might be only one single ice crystal.

Stick Raft

Kids love sticks and these rafts are simple to build and fun to float! This simple activity combines several learning elements, as well as lots of fine-motor skill practice. You can try and float your raft anywhere - from a bowl of water to a bathtub to a small creek to a lake's edge.

TIME: 20 minutes to create
30 minutes to an hour of floating time

SUPPLIES:

*Two thick sticks for the base of the raft

*10-15 sticks of fairly equal length for the raft platform and for the mast

*A large leaf or piece of cloth for the sail

*Twine

*Scissors

*Glue optional

INSTRUCTIONS:

1. Place the two thick sticks parallel to each other at a distance apart that matches the approximate length of the smaller sticks with a little room for overhang.

2. Lay one of the smaller sticks across the two parallel bases. In the two spots where the stick overlaps the base tie tightly with twine, wrapping the twine back and forth several directions.

3. Continue laying the smaller sticks along the two parallel bases. As you add each additional stick connect it to the base with twine. We found it was easiest to connect one entire side first and then tie the other ends of the sticks to the other base. Be sure to pull your twine tight as you tie so that the sticks stay in place.

4. Make your mast using a large leaf or a piece of cloth and a remaining stick. You could use twine to tie a leaf stem to your stick, or you could use a little glue to attach your sail to your mast.

5. Push your mast in between two sticks near the middle of your raft deck. Tie this onto your raft tightly with twine or glue it between the two sticks.

6. Put your raft to the test! Place it in some water and see if it floats.

TAKE IT FURTHER: Experiment with rafts of different shapes and sizes. Create some raft challenges such as furthest distance traveled, fastest moving, carrying the most weight, or surviving pretend stormy weather.

1.

3.

Rainbow Ice Orbs

Sometimes we also call these "ice marbles" and our youngest refers to them as "ice marvels." Whether you call them orbs, marbles, or marvels, these balls of colored ice will dazzle your senses. These provide all sorts of open-ended play opportunities as well.

TIME: 5 minutes to create
24 hours to freeze

SUPPLIES:

*Balloons or orb-shaped ice molds

*Non-toxic food coloring

*Water

INSTRUCTIONS:

1. Add a few drops of non-toxic food coloring to the inside of your balloon or to your ice mold. The more drops of food coloring you add, the darker your ice orbs will be once they are frozen. Be sure to add your food coloring first otherwise you may end up with a large mess on your hands (and your walls).

2. Add water to fill up your balloons or ice molds.

3. Leave to freeze for 24 hours either outside in freezing temperatures or in a freezer.

4. Once frozen, open your ice molds or cut off your balloons (being sure to dispose of them properly). Remember that certain types of food coloring can stain, so be careful handling your ice orbs depending on what you are wearing.

5. Enjoy playing with your ice marbles! They make great hockey pucks or excellent building blocks. Consider using a few of them in your snowball

lantern! Experiment with floating your ice orbs in a bucket of water. Most substances as they get colder, get heavier and tend to sink. Ice is one rare exception to this!

DID YOU KNOW? The Inupiaq of Alaska have many different names for ice. They have a specific word for ice that lasts year after year, another word for ice that has holes in it, a word for slushy ice by the sea, a word for freshwater ice that can be used for drinking, and more.

Ice Ornaments

Here's an easy activity that will keep kids of all ages engaged and entertained. The possibilities here are endless depending on the shapes and sizes of kitchen items you have on hand as well as the loose parts of nature you may have been collecting. Add some bits of color to cold days or make these year round using a freezer!

TIME: 45 minutes of active time
24 hours to freeze

SUPPLIES:

*Any type of receptacle that can hold water and is safe to be frozen. Consider different kitchen items like muffin tins, bundt pans, cake pan molds, pie plates, bowls, etc. We found some different and exciting mold options at the thrift store.

*A collection of nature's loose parts such as flower petals, pinecones, and small sticks

*A pitcher of water

*Twine

*Food coloring, optional

*Dried fruit slices, optional

INSTRUCTIONS:

1. Fill one of your pans with water.

2. Drop in a few drops of food coloring, if desired and give the water a quick stir until the food coloring has completely dissolved.

3. Fill your mold with some of the loose parts you have on hand.

4. If your mold naturally has a cut out in the middle, like a bundt pan, set your pan to freeze either outside or in the freezer. If your mold does not have a cut out in the middle, drape a small piece of twine inside your mold so that both ends are submerged in the water.

When your mold freezes, the handle to hang your ornament will be frozen inside.

5. Once your mold is completely frozen (usually takes about twenty-four hours), remove it from the mold. Add twine to the middle if you used a pan that had an open middle and hang your ornament up from a tree branch. If you are having a hard time removing your mold, carefully place it inside a tray of warm water and it will release quickly.

TAKE IT FURTHER:

*Fill your mold with treats for the animals such as birdseed. Once your mold begins to melt you will have left a tasty treat for nearby critters.

EMOTIONAL HEALTH AND WELL-BEING:

Color is more than a large box of crayons. Our natural world contains the most gorgeous palette of colors and this array of hues can cause subtle changes in our moods and levels of anxiety. When the world is blanketed in whites and browns, an activity like ice ornaments can bring about feelings of rejuvenation through an infusion of color.

4.

1.

Water Play with PVC Pipes

PVC pipes are an inexpensive and simple item to have on hand in order to enhance water play. These can be combined in a wide variety of ways at all sorts of different angles to provide hours of entertainment for children.

TIME: 5 minutes to set-up
Several hours of outside play time

SUPPLIES:

*A few different PVC pipes of various shapes and sizes

*A couple buckets or cups

*Bungee cords or zip ties

*Water

INSTRUCTIONS:

1. Using bungee cords or zip ties attach your pipes to fence posts. Experiment with different lengths of pipes, set at different angles.

2. Use your cups and buckets to pour water through your pipes to collect at the bottom and return to the top and do it all over again!

THE BENEFITS OF MULTI-AGE PLAY: One remarkable thing about nature is that it holds the interest of young to old. Both an infant and a grandparent find water activities delightful and engaging. This activity, like most of the activities in this book, will span the interest-levels of a wide range of ages. A young child may just be interested in pouring water down a tube and seeing the cause-and-effect relationship while an older child may also be interested in angles and speed.

Age-mixing provides exceptional learning opportunities for all who are involved. Older children can learn through teaching and mentoring while younger children learn through observation and new challenges. Multi-age, hands-on experiences provide kids with active, meaningful adventures that expand their knowledge base and help them develop as whole children.

1.

Stacking Ice Bricks

Turn ice into something you can build with! Ice bricks provide limitless play and learning opportunities. In cold weather, ice bricks can be formed into structures simply by spraying with water and allowing that frozen water to act as glue.

TIME: 5 minutes to create
24 hours to freeze

SUPPLIES:

*Loaf pans or rectangular milk or juice cartons that have been washed out

*Non-toxic food coloring, optional

*Water

*Spray bottle, optional

INSTRUCTIONS

1. Fill a loaf pan or rectangular carton with water.

2. Add a few drops of food coloring to reach the desired color.

3. Leave your pan or carton to freeze either in a freezer, or outside when the temperatures have dropped below freezing.

4. Once frozen, release your ice bricks by placing the bottom of the carton or pan in warm water for just a few seconds. This will allow the bottom of your brick to thaw just enough to get it out of its container.

5. Use your ice bricks to create all sorts of things. A spray bottle filled with water will act as glue on a freezing cold day. As you stack your bricks, spray them with an ample amount of water. When the water freezes, your brick structure will be frozen together. Once you are completely finished with your structure, you can also hose the entire thing down with water to make your structure more stable. An extra layer of ice around the outside of your creation will help it stand for a longer period of time.

TAKING IT FURTHER: Can you make an arch, bridge, or maze with your ice bricks? How about a lighted colorful pathway with battery-powered tea lights? You can set the lights in small divots taken out of the earth or snow underneath your bricks. What other architectural innovations can you make using your ice bricks?

good vibes

4.

5.

2.

Water Play with Kitchen Utensils

"Just add water." It's the prevailing advice for a cranky child. There's something about water play that grasps a child's attention and helps to calm them down. Setting up a water play station is easy to do, often with things you already have on hand.

TIME: 20 minutes to set-up
Endless hours of playtime

SUPPLIES:

*A wide variety of kitchen utensils including measuring cups, ladles, serving spoons, slotted spoons, mixing bowls, whisks, pots and pans

*Recycled containers such as yogurt or sour cream tubs or plastic bottles

*Pitchers

*Water dispenser, if possible. This could be as simple as a hose or a water jug with a spigot.

*A few towels, if needed

INSTRUCTIONS:

1. Set out your items on a table or other surface in an appealing way, making sure the water is easily accessible. Beyond the water and kitchen items you could include some other natural elements such as wood boards, bricks, or sticks.

2. Step back and allow for lots of play to happen. Keep a few towels nearby for children to use, if needed.

EMOTIONAL HEALTH AND WELL-BEING:
Many children love the relaxing actions of scooping and pouring water. They enjoy the feeling of the water running through their fingers or watching it run out of the spigot. Kids delight in the sensory experiences of splashing. Water play with kitchen utensils is a tranquil activity meant for children to be absorbed in as they relax into the gentle repetitions of water play.

Snowball Lantern

Snow lanterns originated in Sweden and they are absolutely delightful to make and observe. It's so exciting to head out when it's gotten dark and light up your lantern. In Sweden, these are called snölykta.

TIME: 30 - 60 minutes

SUPPLIES:

*Snow and snowballs

*Tea light and lighter or electric tea light

INSTRUCTIONS:

1. Create snowballs. The more snowballs you have the bigger snowball lantern you can make. Larger snowballs stack easier than smaller ones and you want to make sure that they are fairly uniform in size and packed together well. If you start with a pile of about 75 snowballs you'll be in good shape to make a great lantern.

2. Stack your snowballs in the shape of a pyramid leaving a small space in the back where you'll be able to slip your hand through with a lighted tea light or an electric tea light. Begin with a ring of snowballs. Then add another smaller ring of snowballs on top of your base layer and continue working up with smaller and smaller rings.

3. Since there may be a small element of fire, make sure the space you've created is adequately large to safely slide your hand and candle through in order to set your candle on the ground. If you have access to an electric tea light, you might be able to get by with a smaller opening. Alternatively, you can place your tea light inside your snow lantern just before you've added on the top layer of your pyramid.

TAKE IT FURTHER: Add some color to your snowball lantern by swapping out a snowball or two with one of your colored ice orbs. Or try painting your snowball lantern with a mix of food coloring and water, just like you did with your snow painting. How many snowball lantern varieties can you make?

Supplies

1.

DEVELOPMENTAL BENEFITS KEY

Emotional Benefits

Twig-Bound Journal

Farm Harvest

Colorful Suncatcher

Wildflower Playdough

Ice Ornaments

Water Play with Kitchen Utensils

Social Benefits

Magic Wand

Flower Farm Pretend Play

Mud Kitchen

Pinecone Fairies

Water Play with Kitchen Utensils

Pumpkin Fairy Village

Academic Benefits

Twig Star

Mandala Designs

Sun Prints (Cyanotype)

Memory Game

Monarch Life Cycle

Water Play with PVC Pipes

Physical Benefits

Journey Stick

Lantern Hike

Wax Dipped Leaves

Seasonal Farm Visit

Snowball Lantern

Large Motor Skills Benefits

Forest Teepee

Flower Pounding (Hapa Zome)

Animal Tracking

Stacking Ice Bricks

Fine Motor Skills Benefits

DIY Flower Holder

Seed Starting

Nature Paint Brushes

Nature Glitter

Stick Raft

Flower Pressed Clay Bowls

Creativity and Imagination

Mud Faces

Cardboard Nature Designs

Nature Enhanced Drawings

Pinecone Fairies

Snow Painting

Recommended Resources

These books changed my life and I think they will also change yours! I've read every one cover to cover and often over and over again, with pages that are highlighted and earmarked. These texts will embolden you to slow down, and yet gain more, through nature play. Snag a copy from the library or buy a copy of your own and mark it all up. Any of these would make great baby shower gifts.

Balanced and Barefoot: How Unrestricted Outdoor Play Makes for Strong, Confident, and Capable Children by Angela J. Hanscom

Smart Moves: Why Learning is Not All in Your Head by Carla Hannaford, Ph.D.

Free to Learn: Why Unleashing the Instinct to Play Will Make Our Children Happier, More Self-Reliant, and Better Students for Life by Peter Gray

There's No Such Thing as Bad Weather: A Scandinavian Mom's Secrets for Raising Healthy, Resilient, and Confident Kids (from Friluftsliv to Hygge) by Linda McGurk

The Power of Play: Learning What Comes Naturally by David Elkind, Ph.D.

Simplicity Parenting: Using the Extraordinary Power of Less to Raise Calmer, Happier, and More Secure Kids by Kim John Payne, M.Ed.

How to Raise a Wild Child: The Art and Science of Falling in Love with Nature by Scott D. Sampson

Glow Kids: How Screen Addiction is Hijacking Our Kids - and How to Break the Trance by Nicholas Kardaras, Ph.D.

Learning All the Time: How Small Children Begin to Read, Write, Count, and Investigate the World Without Being Taught by John Holt

Last Child in the Woods: Saving Our Children from Nature-Deficit Disorder by Richard Louv

The following websites are some of my favorite sites to look at for ideas and inspiration.

1000 HOURS OUTSIDE: Balance nature and screen time and get encouragement to help reclaim childhood
www.1000hoursoutside.com

RUN WILD MY CHILD: Helping parents gets kids off screens and outside into nature, one adventure at a time
www.runwildmychild.com

WILDER CHILD: Nature-connected parenting
www.wilderchild.com

MOTHER NATURED: Using nature play to create happier, healthier childhoods
www.mothernatured.com

RAIN OR SHINE MAMMA: There's no such thing as bad weather, only bad clothes
www.rainorshinemamma.com

TANGLEWOOD HOLLOW: Nature inspired materials for the trail and classroom
www.tanglewoodhollow.com

LITTLE PINE LEARNERS: Ideas to inspire people to spend more time learning and playing outdoors with their children or students
www.littlepinelearners.com

BACKWOODS MAMA: Raising Outdoor Kids
www.backwoodsmama.com

TESTIMONIALS

The premise is simple. The impact is profound. If you're joining in on the 1000 Hours Outside journey (you can start any time!) you will have a year filled with simple, but grand memories. Beyond that, your fresh air moments will provide for your family emotionally, socially, physically and cognitively; the perks are vast. I invite you to read some experiences from others all around the world whose lives have benefited from a commitment to the 1000 Hours Outside way of life.

"What if I told you life doesn't have to be the way everyone else does it? That's the deal, folks. That's the challenge. Ginny has started a movement that will transform lives now, and for the future. Clocking our hours outside and making it a priority has radically transformed our family culture and our outlook on education. If I had to cut things from our schedule and our lives, outside time would be the last to go! I'm so thankful for Ginny's heart to normalize childhood, and even adulthood, outside!"
—*SarahRuth, Georgia, USA*

"I've always liked the outdoors but have stuck to the warm pleasant days when everyone else is out. Now, thanks to #1000hoursoutside we are so motivated to spend more glorious hours outside, in all weathers. We have inspired family members too, with and without children to get outside more. The benefits have been huge, the children are sleeping better and talk non-stop about their love for nature. Thank you!"
—*Faye, Portsmouth, United Kingdom*

"The other night before my husband and I went to bed, he asked me how our oldest child's behavior had been lately. I responded that she had a few moments of struggle, but overall really good and no major issues. He responded, 'When your foot was broken every day you messaged me about how overwhelmed you were and how the girls were too much, but since your boot came off, you don't send me those messages anymore' and my realization and response was 'Because we've been

outside' and that's when I realized that this 1000 Hours Outside challenge wasn't for the kids, it was for me."

Motherhood becomes more fun, more tolerable, more full of joy when I put aside everything to just be outside. Even when I'm just the observer in their play. Life doesn't seem so suffocating, even with our lockdown still happening. We always have the forest and the fresh air. I feel like I am finding pieces of myself that I thought were lost and gone forever. I honestly didn't think life could be this happy and fun. 71 hours in and I can never go back to the way things were before this 1000 Hours Outside challenge, nor do I want to. I want to make this priority a life long priority. There's too much negativity in the world, but this, this is pure unaltered joy. This is life in its essence.
—*Lauren, Germany*

"Hi Ginny! I just wanted to say thank you for all the work you do. When I had you as a guest on my podcast last year I never knew what an impact your mission would have on me. After a miscarriage in 2019, your challenge pulled me out of the deep sadness and grief I was feeling. Being intentional about spending outside time with my 3 boys changed my soul as well as my kids. It seems like such a small thing, but in fact has impacted me in more ways that you know. We finished our first year of intentional outside time (lost track of hours), and we are changed. We just had our sweet rainbow baby and she is already racking up hours outside. Thank you."
—*Barbara, Michigan, USA*

"It wasn't until I stumbled upon @1000hoursoutside page on Instagram that I realised how little time we were spending outside. I was literally shocked when we tried her tracker for the first time and we barely made it to 100 hours in three months. But I was determined! Thanks to her lovely and encouraging posts and stories on Instagram we managed to spend 1064 hours outside last year, even with the quarantine due to the pandemic. We learned to love spending time outside, to enjoy the rays of sun on our faces and raindrops wetting our hair, to be mindful of the wonders happening all around us. I'll be forever thankful to Ginny for opening my eyes, my heart and my soul for the outside."
—*Simona, North Macedonia*

"I know it's great to be outside with my kids, but 1000 Hours Outside has given us the right motivation and nudge to really get out there and stay out there! The 1000 Hours Outside Tracker is an awesome tool to celebrate our time outdoors."
—*Stephanie, Lisban, Portugal*

"1000 hours outside made me a better mom! This challenge has taught me to slow down, be patient, and let the children lead."
—*Elanor, Kentville, Nova Scotia*

"I find myself often turning to my husband and saying, 'I wonder what I would have been doing right now, if I hadn't found the Challenge' - how my parenting, my well-being, and my life would have been. It's so strange to think that just a few months ago, the answer would be drastically different than it is today.

The 1000 Hours Outside Challenge has changed my life - and I don't say that lightly. It has changed the way I start and view our days, my overall mood and outlook on life, and most importantly, it has impacted my motherhood journey with my two boys.

Finding this love and devotion to time outside with them has rewarded us with simply that - time.

In a world and society where we unknowingly lose seconds, minutes, hours and days to the powerful screens we hold in our hands, finding this challenge was a wake up call that shook me to my core. Through the 1000 Hours Outside challenge, the true power of time in Nature has given my family and I a chance to reawaken all our senses, rekindle sacred family time, and squeeze all those precious moments out of every day. Thank you. Thank you. Thank you."
—*Kyla, Ottawa, Ontario, Canada*

"Paradigm shifting. That's probably the best way to describe what taking this challenge on and becoming part of the 1000 Hours Outside community has done for our family. While we've always considered ourselves "outdoors' people" we had definitely fallen into a comfort trap; with a three year old and a 10 month old for awhile the juggle was real, and when a particularly hard day went by with too much screentime we knew we needed an alternative.

The 1000 Hours Outside Challenge gently reminded my husband and I what the outdoors meant to us when we were young, and that with a little bit of prep we didn't have to let it fall by the wayside. We had been so focused on the big adventures adults plan (trips and holidays) we forgot about the little everyday excursions children require to thrive.

We're more prepared for the daily occurrences of puddle jumping, pockets full of treasures, and all the mud and muck our three-year old can find. Now there's always an 'adventure kit' and change of clothes for everyone, just in case we find ourselves on an impromptu excursion. We welcome every moment we get to add to our tracker. 1000 Hours Outside has truly changed our family's approach to life in such an incredible way, and I'm so excited for our boys and all the hours of adventure still in front of them."
—*Anjuli, NSW, Australia*

THANK YOU!

To the Fearsome Five, thanks for walking this road right alongside me. This truly is a family book! Thank you for being the world's cutest models and for pitching in extra during this busy season. I hope you always jump head first into the unknown and tackle life with everything you've got.

To Josh, thanks for holding down the fort while we inserted all sorts of additional elements into our day-to-day routine. You are an expert at rummaging up kid's clothing with no logos, finding step stools, and piecing together dinners on a moment's notice. We're doing it!

To the four lovely and loving grandparents in our life, Bubby, Zeydie, Nana and Papa. What an absolute treat to have you be a part of this book. Thank you for laying the foundation of embracing real-world moments during our own childhoods and then joining in on this book with huge smiles on your faces despite frigid Michigan temperatures. Above all else, thank you for being such doting and attentive parents and grandparents.

To our beautiful friends, thank you for allowing your children to be a part of this experience and for helping out considerably throughout the activities. Thank you, Angie for your photographic eye and for Tank. Thank you, Nellie for understanding it all. I'm so grateful for our matching families. Thank you, Missie for your remarkable hair. Thank you, Lisa for the incredible early childhood years we had together and for the memories we continue to make. Thank you, Julie for our awesome day in the woods filled with vibrant leaves, beeswax, soup and pamplemousse. And thank you most of all to the incredible children whom I am so privileged to know and to watch grow up: Ellie and Ellie, Jonelle, JP, Lillian, Caleb, Adeline, Isaac, Owen, Eli, Marcus, Mason, and Mylie.

To my mother, you are the breath I breathe. During the final hours, you stepped up to edit and encourage and bring this book to life. I love you! Cal-Five-Plus, the Red-Winged Blackbird was a last minute addition, just for you. XOXO

And to the 1000 Hours Outside families who are day-by-day spreading the message around the globe that nature play offers children and adults more than we could ever imagine. We stand as the gatekeepers of our time and of our calendars and I believe we are seeing a seismic shift back toward the simple, necessary components of childhood.

GINNY YURICH

ABOUT THE AUTHOR

Ginny Yurich is a Michigan-based, homeschooling mama of five kids 12 years old and under and the founder of 1000 Hours Outside. She recently moved with her husband and kids to a small hobby farm and they are learning the ropes, with all sorts of new endeavors. When the stars align you might find Ginny reading or playing the piano but most of her time these days is spent hanging out with her children, and she wouldn't have it any other way.

Ginny is a thought-leader in the world of nature-based play and its benefits for children (and adults). Nature immersion changed the entire parenting journey for Ginny and she has been sharing her experiences about a lifestyle that prioritizes nature time at **www.1000HoursOutside.com.** Ginny has a BS in Mathematics and a Masters Degree in Education from the University of Michigan and she is also a speaker, author and illustrator. Her children's book, The Little Farmhouse in West Virginia was published in 2019.

The 1000 Hours Outside movement spans the globe and many people from all walks of life look to Ginny for inspiration as well as practical tips on how to put down the screens and get outside. There is a very active social media community and you can use #1000HoursOutside across social media channels like facebook and Instagram to find like-minded families who have chosen to slow down and yet gain more through nature play.

"What the child finds worthy, is worthy."
—Ginny Yurich

THE END

JOIN THE MOVEMENT AT

1000HOURSOUTSIDE.COM